AMERICAN MARITIME
DOCUMENTS

AMERICAN MARITIME DOCUMENTS 1776-1860

ILLUSTRATED AND DESCRIBED

DOUGLAS L. STEIN

DOUGLAS L. STEIN *holds degrees in American History from Bradley University and from Illinois State University. He has written articles on maritime subjects, and speaks frequently to museum, library and educational groups about the significance of maritime documents. He is the author of* A Guide to the Manuscript Collections of the G.W. Blunt White Library, *published by Mystic Seaport Museum, and is Curator of Manuscripts at the Seaport's G.W. Blunt White Library.*

This monograph has been published through a generous grant from the Andrew W. Mellon Foundation.

CONTENTS

To CONNIE
and the KIDS

The impetus for this book came from my interest in maritime history and a desire to learn more about the documents I work with as Curator of Manuscripts at Mystic Seaport Museum. Its publication, however, is the result of several individuals, organizations, and groups that provided support and encouragement along the way.

I take great pleasure in acknowledging my sincere thanks to Mystic Seaport Museum for allowing me the time to research and put together this book under what our Director of Publications is fond of calling a "research without guilt" program. I must also thank the Fellows of the G.W. Blunt White Library, a dedicated group of individuals whose active interest in, and financial support of, this publication was so important.

Virginia Coope and Dorothy Tower have worked with me for many years as volunteers in the Manuscript Collection. They played a valuable role in the description and identification of many document s found in this book. So have several research assistants, provided through both the Williams College-Mystic Seaport Maritime Studies Program, and the Munson Institute Summer Internship in Museum Studies. I offer particular thanks to Amy Butler and Mary Ellen Knapka. The many hours they spent examining reference materials and writing up drafts of document descriptions really moved the project out of the research phase and into production. The quality of their work was superb.

The Peabody Museum in Salem, Massachusetts, and the Rhode Island Historical Society in Providence permitted the use of important documents from their collections. I offer my thanks particularly to John Koza at the Peabody, and Cynthia Bendroth at Rhode Island Historical. This book has been made better by their involvement with it.

Of great assistance also have been my colleagues at other institutions, especially the members of our Maritime Librarians group: Virginia Adams and Judith Downey of the New Bedford Whaling Museum; Nathan Lipfert of Maine Maritime Museum; Ann Wilcox from the Philadelphia Maritime Museum; Ben Trask and Tom Crew at Mariner's Museum, Newport News, Virginia; David Hull, San Francisco Maritime Museum, and Mr. L. Byrne Waterman. Their interest in this project, as well as their advice and suggestions, have helped make this book possible.

Here at Mystic, Paul O'Pecko, our Reference Librarian, was instrumental in tracking down essential sources for the accurate identification of particular documents. Gerald Morris, Director of Publications, believed in the project from the beginning, and never lacked ways to encourage me to continue on whenever my enthusiasm waned. Mary Anne Stets and the Photo Lab staff produced the quality photographs so important to this book, and Andy German, Publications Dept. Editor, picked up several loose ends and got the whole thing done. And finally, I must thank Connie Stein, Publications Assistant, for hours of proofing copy, creating revised drafts, checking sources, etc. Yes, I am Connie's husband, even after all those hours of proofing copy, etc.

INTRODUCTION

I could have used a book like this twenty years ago. Back then I was fresh out of graduate school, and processing my first maritime manuscript collections. Although I possessed an interest in maritime history and some knowledge of nautical terms, I had never come face to face with a Bottomry Bond or an Enrollment Certificate.

I soon discovered that the study of maritime history exposed one to many documents unique to this field, and that they must be accurately identified and interpreted by those of us entrusted with their management. Marine dictionaries and nautical encyclopedia were obvious sources, but a comprehensive monograph on maritime documents would have better served the purpose.

Now Mystic Seaport Museum has published such a volume, a book written to assist researchers in identifying specific documents and papers, which are unique in some measure to the conduct of America's shipping industry through the first half of the nineteenth century. It is intended as a reference tool for students, educators, manuscripts dealers and collectors, librarians, archivists, curators, and anyone else who may require a better understanding of maritime documents.

The period between the years 1776 and 1860 saw the development of Federal legislation designed to regulate and protect our maritime commerce. The documents generated by these statutes were issued through the United States Customs Service, an agency of the Treasury Department created in 1789, and by the U.S. Consular Service at foreign ports.

The variety of Customs and Consular forms are well represented in this guide, comprising over half of the documents described. The various Licenses, Certificates, Passports, and Permits, etc., offer insight into how the government sought to develop American shipping, and create revenue by controlling the transportation and sale of imported goods. In addition, numerous Bonds and Oaths have been included, showing the primary method employed to insure compliance with the various conditions under which a particular document was obtained. Other documents relative to the protection and safety of American seamen and passengers are also illustrated.

Business documents representing some unique aspect of the maritime industry have not been overlooked. Marine insurance policies and related papers are discussed in detail. The Charter Party is also described, along with some of the more familiar and maritime-related receipts, Bills of Lading and Manifests, etc.

We have been liberal enough with our definition of "document" so that we might include other relevant pieces of potential interest. Represented here are the "Morning Star" Contribution Certificate and the Freight Circular. Sailing Cards, although not manuscripts, have also been included, since they are interesting instruments of maritime commerce, valued by both researchers and collectors.

Any items that are specifically associated with naval matters have been excluded from this work. Hence United States naval commissions, reports, logbooks, etc., do not appear. Also, papers and documents usually considered common to any business or industry; i.e. ledgers, account books, payroll records, statements, etc., fall outside the scope of this volume, as do family papers such as letters and diaries, deeds, wills, and other similar pieces.

Many of the documents illustrated are printed forms, some are entirely handwritten, but nearly all possess a certain degree of consistency in form or content which makes them unique and identifiable. Some pieces are remarkably standardized, and changed very little during the time they were used. The Mediterranean Passport and the Sea Letter, for example, are documents whose physical appearance remained relatively unaltered.

Other documents and forms were frequently printed by local print shops near the ports where they were used, a situation which produced a variety of styles for Manifests, Articles of Agreement, Clearance Certificates, etc.

The examples found in this work have been taken primarily from the manuscripts collection at Mystic Seaport Museum. This collection contains more than five hundred thousand pieces, is extensively cataloged, and represents a major research source for the study of American maritime history. We have also solicited documents from other institutions in order to produce the best or most appropriate illustration for every piece described.

The illustrations are intended to assist in identifying these documents, and they are presented in a way that best satisfies this purpose. In most cases the photos have not been cropped. Instead the entire piece is represented, which allows the reader to better visualize the format or composition of that particular item. Larger documents have been reduced only to the point where they can be properly represented on a single page, while some small items were enlarged a bit for the same reason. When dimensions of a document are important, they have been included in the physical description. In other instances I have indicated that a piece varied considerably in size, so its measurements are of little value in the identification process.

Finally, this volume does not pretend to include examples of every document used by the American maritime industry during this period, but we have made an effort to provide a large selection of the most important and/or frequently found documents in collections of maritime manuscripts. Each piece is illustrated and described, so that the reader may easily and accurately identify a particular document, or perhaps better understand its significance as a research source. We trust that this volume will be a useful addition to maritime historiography, and prove of value to those who use it.

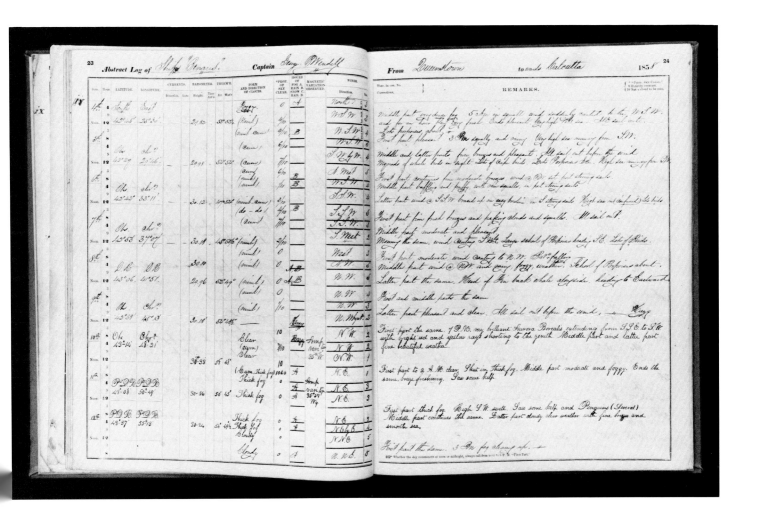

Occasionally a shipmaster *might extract specific kinds of information from his vessel's log-book and record them in a separate volume, sometimes called an Abstract Log. Possibly the kind most often found in maritime collections is the Abstract Log of navigational data recommended by the Maritime Conference at Brussels in 1853 and formulated in part by Lt. Matthew Fontaine Maury, USN. (illustrated). These logs were maintained by the master or mate during the voyage, and then returned to the National Observatory in Washington, D.C., in exchange for the use of Maury's Wind and Current Charts.*

15

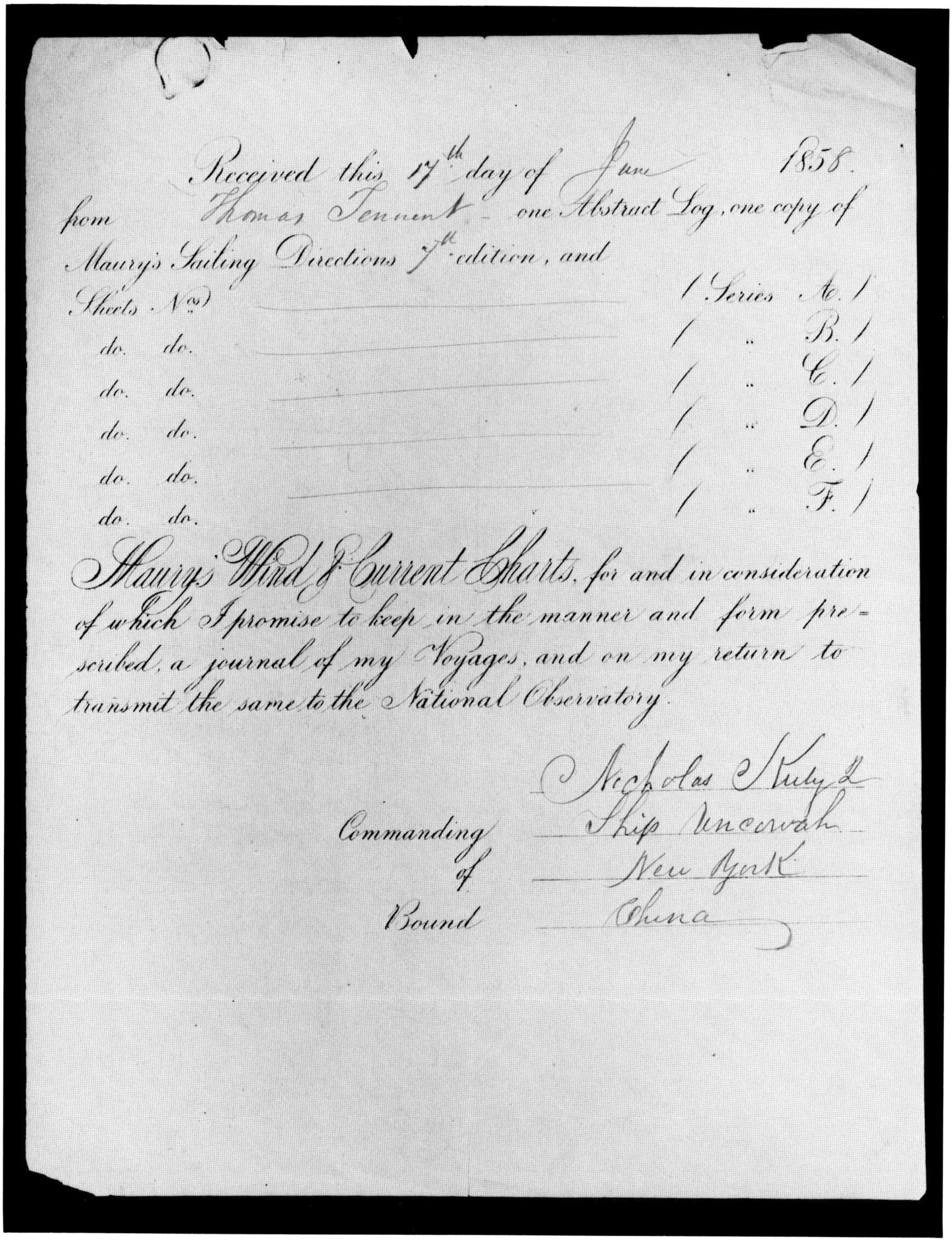

Received this 17th day of June 1858. from Thomas Tennent one Abstract Log, one copy of Maury's Sailing Directions 7th edition, and Sheets No)

				1 Series	A. 1
do.	do.			1 "	B. 1
do.	do.			1 "	C. 1
do.	do.			1 "	D. 1
do.	do.			1 "	E. 1
do.	do.			1 "	F. 1

Maury's Wind & Current Charts, for and in consideration of which I promise to keep in the manner and form pre-scribed, a journal of my Voyages, and on my return to transmit the same to the National Observatory.

Commanding
of
Bound

Nicholas Skuly 2
Ship Uncowah
New York
China

Receipt for Maury's Sailing Directions, and Wind & Current Charts: *This form, signed by the shipmaster, acknowledged his receipt of Maury's Abstract Log and the related guide book, entitled* Sailing Directions, *plus 6 charts. All this was free of charge, provided the master kept the Abstract Log "in the manner and form prescribed," and returned it to the National Observatory so that the data could be used in future chart editions.*

Often a printed document, varying in size and format. Early examples averaged about 16" x 20" – however, by the 1860s, 23" x 18" was a common size. On the front of the document were the conditions agreed to between a vessel's managers and the crew. Below this was a column for crew members' signatures, in addition to columns for such data as station, birth place, age, height, wages, hospital money, time of discharge, etc. The number and designations of these columns varied from one document to another. "United States Of America" is often printed prominently on the frontside, and engraved ships, eagles, etc., are frequently found on both sides of the Articles. After 1790 the backside quite often presented printed abstracts of all Federal laws currently in force relative to seamen's protection and the conduct of officers and crew while at sea. There was also a place set aside for the crew to sign for receipt of their wages at the end of the voyage. Customs or consular stamps and seals were also present.

By a Congressional Act in 1790, Articles of Agreement was a document required of every vessel sailing for a foreign port and for any vessel, of 50 tons or more, bound to any domestic port, except to one in an adjoining state. Fishermen engaged in the fisheries also had to sign shipping articles, and were entitled to the same privileges and subject to the same regulations as sailors. The document contained the signatures of the master and every member of the crew (or his mark), and was considered to be a separate contract for each person signing. It provided legal evidence not only as to the nature and length of the voyage, but as to the duties to be performed and wages due. A copy of the Articles, certified by the collector, had to be taken aboard ship by the master, and was to be produced, when required, before any consul or commercial agent to whom a complaint was made. Since a new Articles of Agreement was required for each voyage (and they were not recalled by the Customs Service) these documents are commonly found in maritime collections. They rank among the more valuable and comprehensive research sources, providing important information for a great number of marine subjects.

I T is agreed between the Mafter, Seamen, and Mariners of the *Sloop Nabby* bound for *Hispaniola* that in Confideration of the Sums as monthly Wages affixed to our Names, that the faid Seamen and Mariners will perform a Voyage from *Norwich* to *Hispaniola* and back to *Norwich* promifing hereby to obey the lawful Orders and Commands of the faid Mafter, or of other Officers of the faid *Sloop* and faithfully to do and perform the Duty of Seamen, as required by faid Mafter, by Night and by Day, on Board the faid *Sloop* or in her Boats, and on no Account or Pretence whatever, to go on Shore without Leave firft obtained from the Mafter or Commander of faid *Sloop* hereby agreeing that forty-eight Hours Abfence without fuch Leave fhall be deemed a total Defertion ; and in Cafe of Difobedience, Neglect, Pillage, or Embez-zlement or Defertion, the faid Mariners do forfeit their Wages, together with all their Goods, Chat-tels, &c. on Board faid Ship ; hereby for themfelves, Heirs Executors or Adminiftrators, renoun-cing all Right and Title to the fame. And the Mafter of faid *Sloop* hereby promifes and obliges himfelf, upon the above Conditions, to pay the faid monthly Wages, as fet againft the Names of the Seamen and Mariners of the faid *Sloop* upon return of faid *Sloop* to the Port of *Norwich* on her Arrival at faid *Norwich* the Port of her Difcharge *one half in Cafh & the other half in goods*

I N Teftimony of our free Affent, Confent and Agreement to the Premifes we have hereunto fet our Hands, the Day and Date affixed to our Names.

Time of Entry	Men's Names	Quality	Witnefs of our Signing	Advance Wages	Wages per Mo. or Run	Whole Wages	Time of Difcharge
July 3	Elisha Coit	Mafter			2	3.14.8	Oct 29th 1787
2d July	Elias ... Myte				2.15	10.14.8	Do
July 3	... Othen	Cooper			3.10	13.0.6	Do 9th
July 6	Jofeph Smith	Seaman	Simeon Bree	2.0.0	2.0.0	Do	Do 29th
June 28	...	do	do		2.2.0	2.9.0	Do 25th
July 5	Wm S Billing	do			2	2.6.8	Do 25th
July 3	William Powell				1.4	4.2.9	Do 29th
June 28					2.2	8.12	
July 9th				Cafh 8.12	2.4		Cufhing 25th

Articles of Agreement were being used even before the Act of 1790. This example, June - July 1787, was essentially a private contract between the vessel's owners and each member of the crew who signed the Articles. There are no signatures of port officials, and obviously no references to compli-ance with existing regulatory laws. The document is similar in size and style, however, to the more standardized forms that existed during the early 1800s.

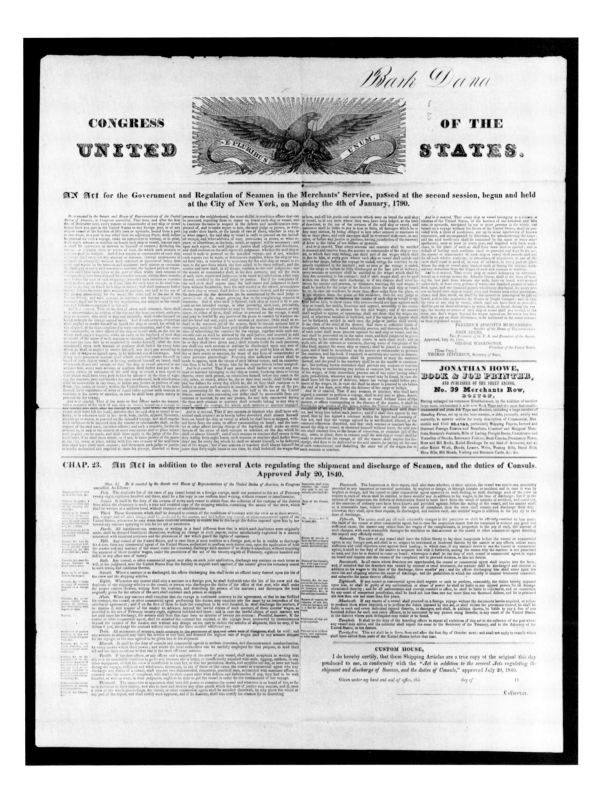

The reverse side of the Articles often contained sections of Federal legislation relative to seamen's protection, and the conduct of American vessels towards their crew members. The example illustrated here is typical of those in use during the mid-nineteenth century.

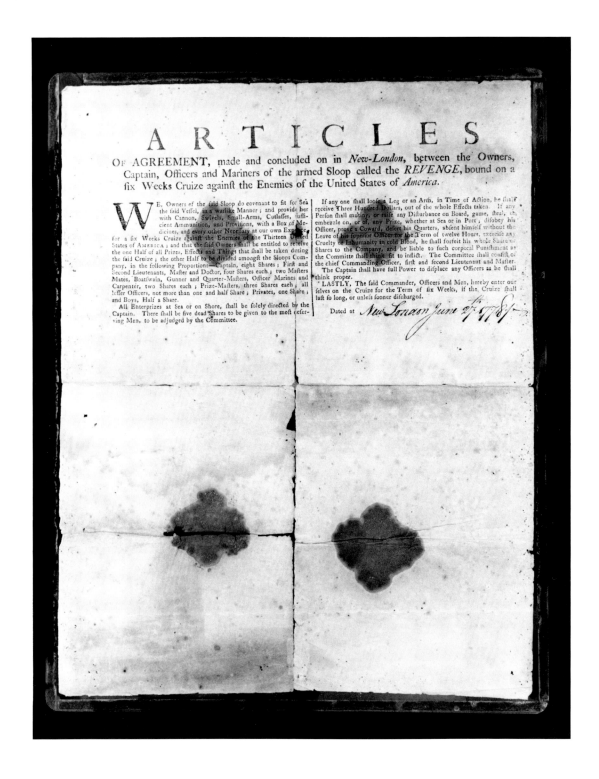

This Articles of Agreement *was part of the documentation required by the owners of the Privateer* Revenge, *for a cruise against the British. The printed format is unique, since these documents were usually completely handwritten. Note that it was printed specifically for the sloop* Revenge, *and indicated that the vessel was to sail, "...against the Enemies of the Thirteen United States of America...," for a period not to exceed six weeks. Although dated at New London, Connecticut, on 27 June 1778, the Articles were evidently never executed, since no signatures of crew members or officers, etc., appear in the space provided.*

A printed document. These certificates were usually printed locally for use by the port's customs officers, and thus vary a great deal in size and format. Frequently the words, "Bill of Health" do not appear, but the name of the customs district issuing the Bill is often prominently displayed. Some documents exhibit decorative engravings, while all provide spaces for the vessel's name and master, cargo, destination, and number of persons aboard. Signatures of the Collector and the Naval Officer are present.

By the end of the eighteenth century a Bill of Health was required as part of a ship's papers, and certified the status of contagious disease at the port during the time of departure. A clean bill of health indicated that no plague or infectious disorders were known to exist. A suspected bill indicated rumors of disease, although it had not yet appeared, and a foul bill certified that the port of departure was infected at the time the ship sailed. A clean bill of health was by far the most common, and these are often found in maritime collections.

No. *1.*

United States of America.

DISTRICT OF *Kennebunk.*

To all to whom these Presents shall come :— I, the Collector of the Port of *Kennebunk* . . . . do, by the tenor of these Presents, certify and make known, that the Captain, Officers, Seamen and Passengers of the *Brig* called *Traveller* . . . . laden with

Lumber

and of which *Joseph Perkins Jur* . is Captain; consisting of *eight* . . Officers and Seamen, and *no* . Passengers, now ready to proceed on a voyage to *Madeira* and elsewhere beyond sea, are all in good health.

AND I DO FURTHER CERTIFY, That no Plague, or other contagious or dangerous disease, at present exists in this Port or in its vicinity; *and that there is no public Agent or Consul of any foreign power residing in or near this place*.

GIVEN under my hand and the Seal of the Custom-House at *Kennebunk* . the *second* day of *March*, in the year of our Lord One thousand eight hundred and *ten*, and in the *34th* year of the Independence of the said States.

Joseph Storer, Collector.

Bill of Health signed by the Collector at the Port of Kennebunk, 2 March 1810. "No 1" indicates that it was the first one to be issued that year.

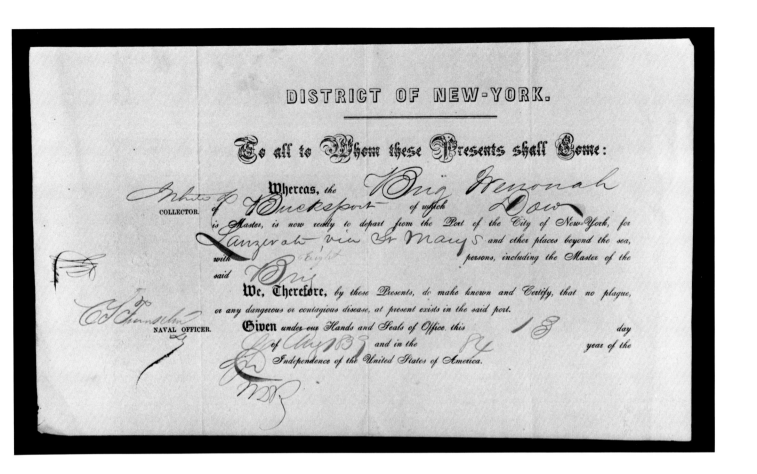

Bill of Health from the Port of New York, *containing the signatures of the Collector and Naval Officer, August 13, 1859.*

BILL OF LADING

A one-page printed form varying in size and style, 8" x 6" to 5" x 11", representing approximate common measurements. Usually began, "Shipped in Good Order And (Well Conditioned) Condition, by..." Small engravings of sailing vessels are often present. Revenue stamps frequently appear, and a handwritten receipt of goods by the consignee is sometimes found on the reverse side.

The Bill of Lading was signed by the master, acknowledging receipt of the cargo described on the document. It also reaffirms his obligation to deliver the goods to the consignee or his order as detailed in the Charter Party. The amount of cargo taken in is indicated, and any identifying marks are included in the description. There were usually three or four copies of a Bill of Lading. One was delivered to the master, another kept by the shipper, and one was sent to the consignee. Bills of Lading were considered part of a private transaction between the owner of the goods and the master, and did not provide the same degree of authenticity as the Charter Party or the Manifest. Bills of Lading are common maritime documents which can provide valuable information about the transportation of various cargoes and the business of shipping.

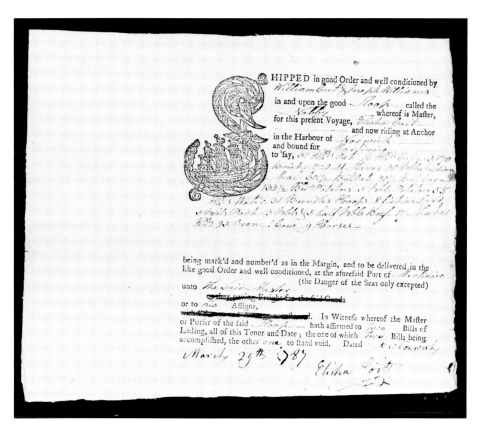

Bill of Lading for shipment of "One Trunk," from New York to Georgetown, and consigned to James Madison, Secretary of State, September, 1802.

Bill of Lading for general cargo to the West Indies, March, 1787. Since goods were not consigned, the master was responsible for finding buyers when he arrived.

BILL OF SALE

Printed document, occasionally displayed small decorative engraving. Originally one page, approximately 7 1/2" x 12"; later (*ca.* 1850s) evolved into a four-page format, approximately 8" x 13," and was often printed on the blue-gray paper common to the period. Customs seal might also be found.

A Bill of Sale is the true and proper instrument of title to a ship to which all maritime courts looked for proof of ownership. The usual evidence of such property is the Bill of Sale along with the register or enrollment. Accordingly, a copy of the registry or Enrollment Certificate is usually incorporated into the Bill of Sale document. A Bill of Sale provided the following information: The name and description of the vessel, when and where it was built, the names of the buyer and seller, the portion sold and the purchase price, the place of registry or enrollment, the names of all current owners, the number of the new register or enrollment along with a reference to the previous certificate which this particular Bill of Sale invalidated. By the act of 29 July 1850, custom houses were made the recording agency for all papers affecting the title to vessels. Bills of Sale are frequently found in maritime collections. Since it was not unusual for someone who was otherwise not directly connected to the maritime industry to own shares in one or more ships, these documents occasionally appear in other business or private papers. They are important sources for maritime research.

FOR REGISTERED VESSELS. McSpedon & Baker, Stationers and Printers, 25 Pine street.

To all whom these Presents shall come—GREETING:

Know ye, That I Milton G. Smith of the City, County and State of New York, Owner of One Sixteenth of the Ship or vessel, called the Electric of New York of the burthen of 1273 81/95 tons, or thereabouts, for and in consideration of the sum of Three Thousand One hundred & seventy five dollars lawful money of the United States of America, to me in hand paid before the sealing and delivery of these presents, by John H. Brower and Benjamin B. Blydenburgh Copartners the receipt whereof I do hereby acknowledge; and am therewith fully satisfied, contented and paid, have bargained and sold, and by these presents do bargain and sell, unto the said John H. Brower & Benjamin B. Blydenburgh their executors, administrators and assigns, One Sixteenth of the said Ship or vessel; together with One Sixteenth of the mast, bowsprit, sails, boat, anchors, cables, and all other necessaries thereunto appertaining and belonging; the certificate of the Register of which said Ship or vessel is as follows, to wit:

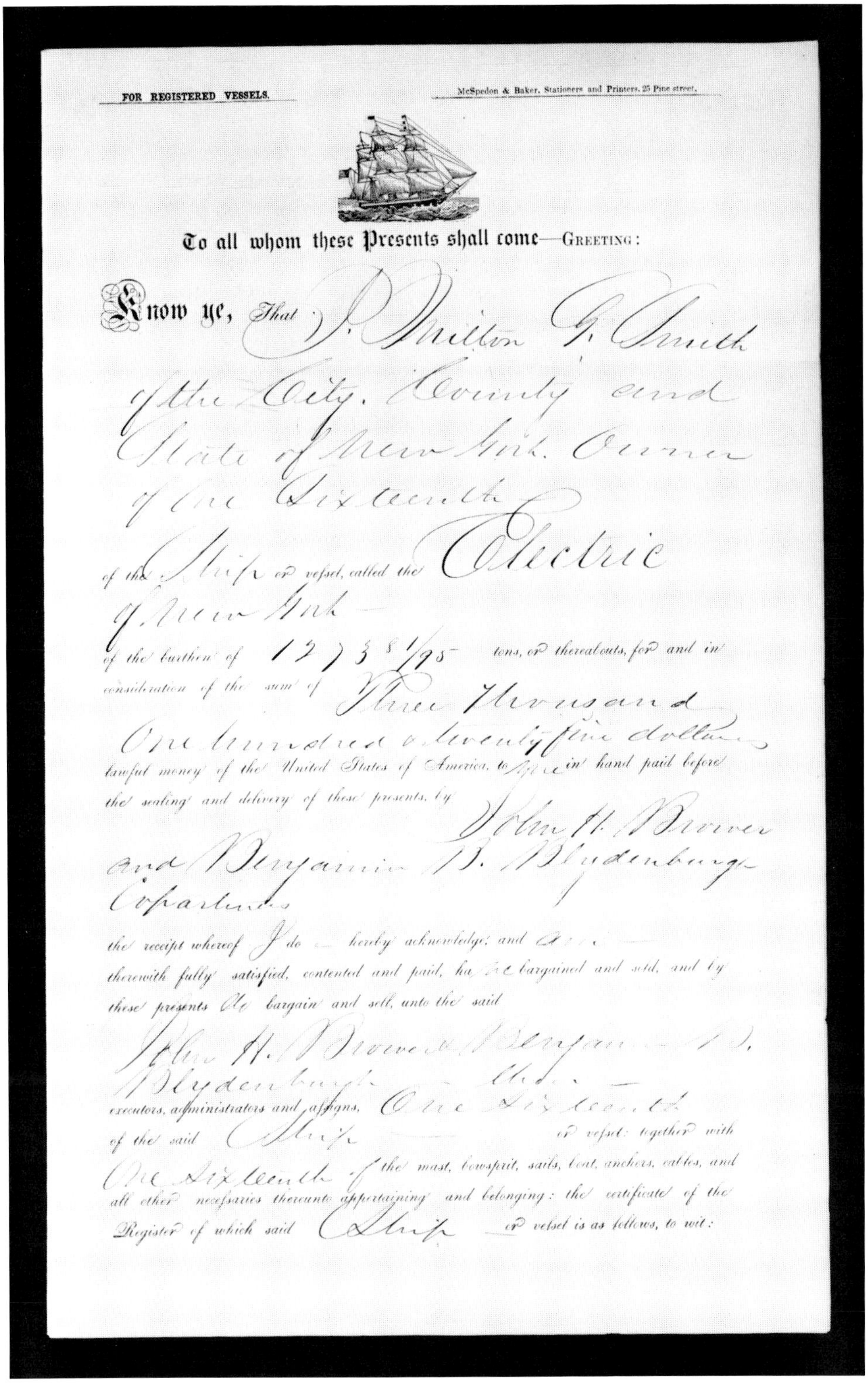

The four-page format for a Bill of Sale *was commonly used by the mid-nineteenth century. The first page, illustrated here, is typical of the format and language found on these documents.*

Bond For Duties

MAN. 2

KNOW all Men by these presents, That we Daniel W. Lord & Ivory Jefferds of Kennebunkport in the State of Maine

are held and firmly bound unto the UNITED STATES OF AMERICA, in the sum of Three Thousand dollars to be paid to the said United States; for payment whereof, we bind ourselves, our heirs, executors, and administrators, jointly and severally, firmly by these Presents. Sealed with our seals. Dated this Twenty sixth day of January in the forty-67 year of the Independence of the said United States, and in the year of our Lord one thousand eight hundred and twenty five.

GOOD FOR 640 22/100 Dolls.

THE CONDITION OF THIS OBLIGATION IS SUCH, THAT IF THE ABOVE-BOUNDEN Lord & Jefferds

or either of them or either of their heirs, executors, or administrators, shall and do, on or before the twenty sixth day of October next, well and truly pay, or cause to be paid, unto the Collector of the Customs for the District of Kennebunk, for the time being the sum of Fifteen hundred dollars and cents, or the amount of the duties to be ascertained as due, and arising on certain goods, wares, and merchandise, entered by the above-bounden D. W. Lord as imported in the Sch Warren, Ivory Jefferds master, from Porto Cabello as per entry, dated this date then the above obligation to be void, otherwise to remain in full force and virtue.

Sealed and delivered in the presence of

Geo. Wheelwright

Danl. W. Lord

I. Jefferds

Paid 29th October 1825

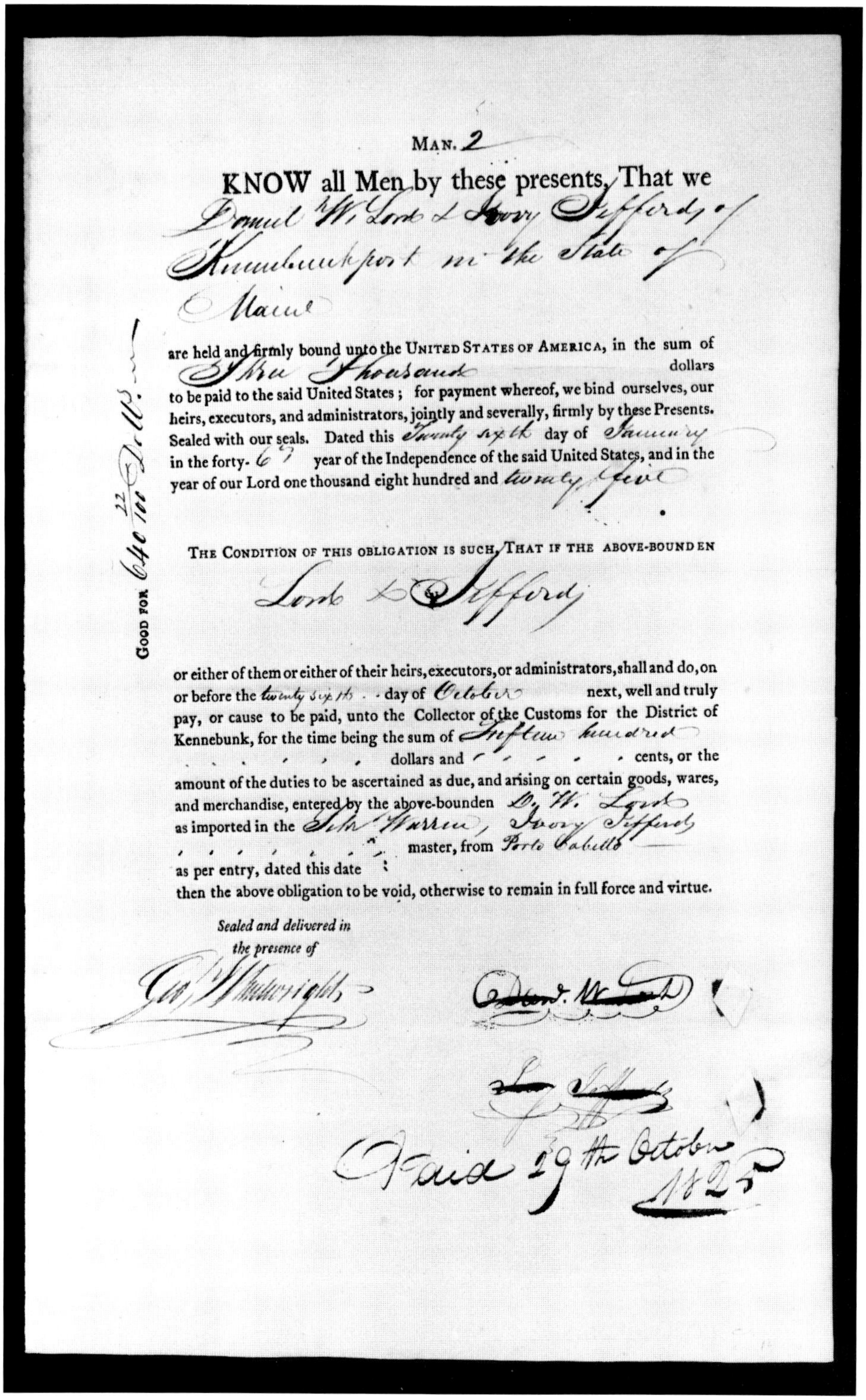

Bonds for Duties on imported goods *were fairly standardized printed documents with little or no ornamentation. If the duties for an imported cargo were over $200, the owner or consignee of the cargo could either pay immediately or sign this document, which bonded him for twice the amount of the duties. Blunt's 1837 edition of* Shipmaster's Assistant *states that the regulations at that time indicated one-half the duties were to be paid within three months and the balance in six months from the importation date. The Bond illustrated here states that Messrs. Lord and Jefferds are bonded to the U.S. Government for three thousand dollars if the duties on their goods, amounting to fifteen hundred dollars, are not paid within nine months from 26 January 1825.*

To obtain clearance papers during the early decades of the nineteenth century, owners and/or masters often had to swear that their vessel would not engage in trade with particular nations. In addition they were required to sign a Bond, sometimes totaling over 75 thousand dollars, to insure their compliance with all existing laws governing foreign trade. During the embargo, in effect from 25 December 1807 to 1 March 1809, permission for foreign voyages was particularly restricted. Later, during the era of the Non-Intercourse Act, trade with France and England was prohibited. If the Bond were violated, the collector could initiate legal action against the Bond holders, and if the libel case was successfully prosecuted by the District Courts, the amount of the Bond, plus any additional expenses, was forfeited to the United States.

Bonds For Foreign Voyages

Know all Men by these Presents, That we George Williamson of the City County State of New York — Sole owner , and Edward Williams of New London master of the vessel, called the Juliana burthen 294 & 51/95 — tons and Samuel H Eakin John Harvey & David Hunt

are held and firmly bound to the United States of America, in the full and just sum of Seventy five thousand Ninety & 40/100 Dollars, to which payment well and truly to be made, we bind ourselves, our heirs, executors and administrators, jointly and severally firmly by these presents. Sealed with our seals, and dated this twenty sixth day of October in the year of our Lord one thousand eight hundred and Nine

Whereas, The said vessel is bound to a foreign place to wit, to Fayal

Now therefore, The condition of this obligation is such that if the said vessel shall not proceed to any port or place with which commercial intercourse is not thus permitted, nor be directly or indirectly engaged, during the voyage, in any trade with such port or place: then this obligation shall be void, and otherwise the same shall remain in full force and virtue.

Sealed and Delivered in the presence of

George Williamson

Edward Williams

Saml. H. Eakin

John Harvey

David Hunt

Bond For A Foreign Voyage: *This document indicates that the owner, master, and three others, were bonded to the United States for the sum of $75,090.40, in order to insure compliance with all existing trade and embargo laws by the ship* Juliana *during her voyage to Fayal, 26 October 1809. Bonds might vary somewhat from one port of issue to another, although much of the language within these documents remained the same. One might also find handwritten bonds, which would most often be record copies. Originals might frequently contain the usual customs signatures, stamps or seals, and could also have related papers (i.e. Manifests, Clearance Papers, etc.) attached to them. The example illustrated here was the Collector's copy.*

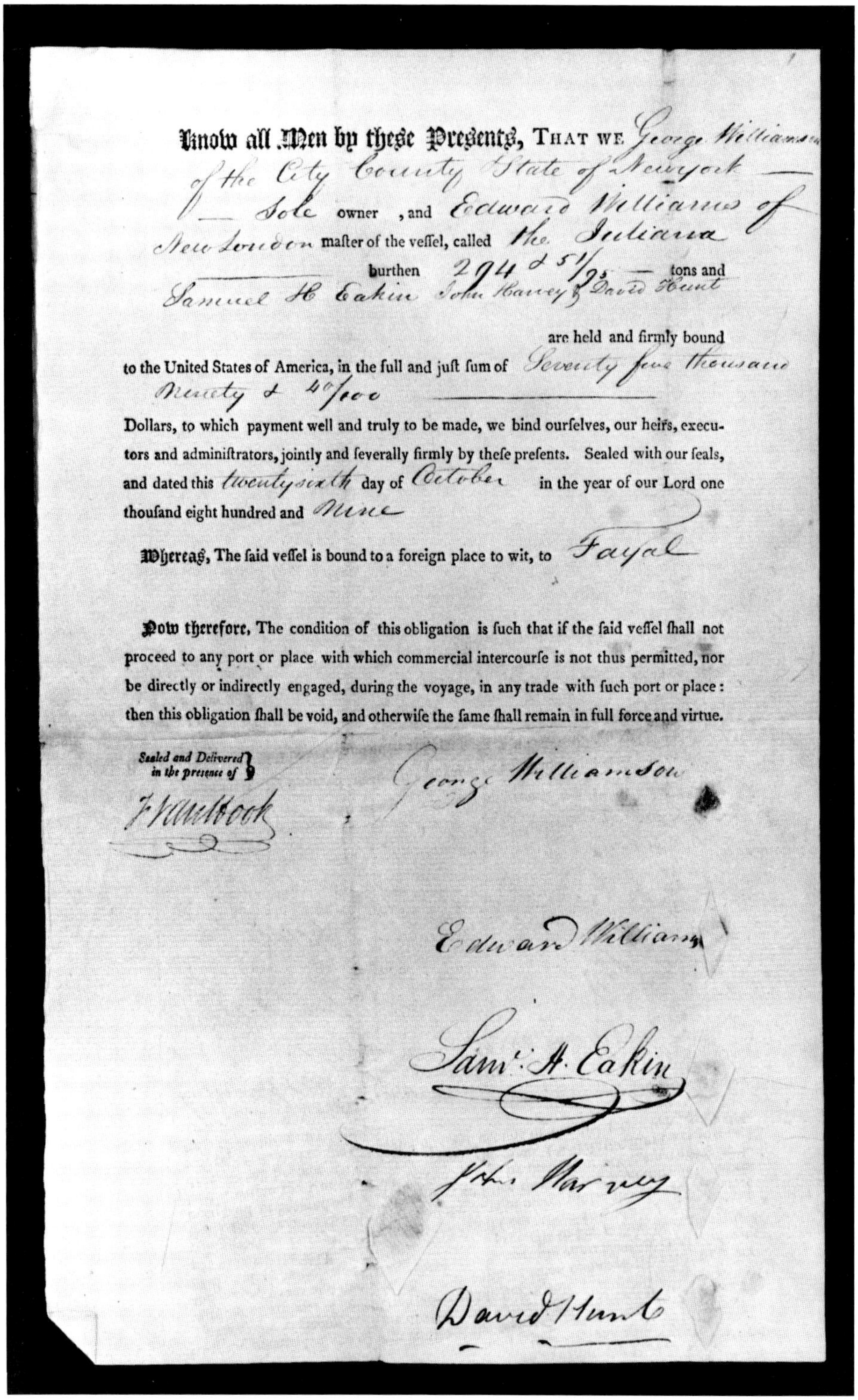

District of New-York—Port of New-York.

TO ALL TO WHOM THESE PRESENTS *shall come, or may concern:* GREETING.

Know Ye, *That* Isaac Smith of Brooklyn State of New York *master of the* Schoon *or vessel called the* Polly *burthen* Twenty three 23/95 *tons, having given bond to the United States of America, in the penal sum of* four thousand six hundred *dollars, with the condition that the said* Schoon *or vessel shall not be employed in any foreign trade during the continuance of the act entitled " An act laying an Embargo on all ships and vessels in the ports and harbours of the United States,"* **Permission** *is hereby given to the said* Schoon *or vessel, called the* Polly *of* Wallabout *to depart this port, and pursue her lawful business.*

GIVEN *under my* **Hand** *and* **Seal** *of office, at the* **Custom House,** *this* Twenty seventh *day of* June *in the Year one thousand eight hundred and* Eight

Bonded Voyage Permit: *Enrolled vessels were also bonded, to insure that the "...vessel shall not be employed in any foreign trade during the continuance of the act entitled 'An Act laying an Embargo on all ships and vessels in the ports and harbours of the United States'..." The customs document illustrated here indicates that the Schooner* Polly *has been bonded in the sum of $4,600.00, and can now "...depart this port, and pursue her lawful business," New York 27 June 1808. Document contains the signature of the Deputy Collector, and a customs seal.*

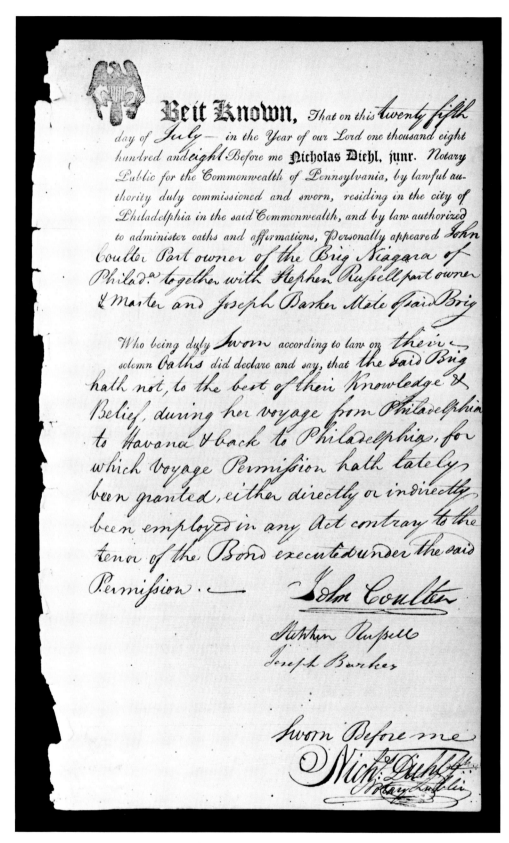

Be it Known, That on this twenty fifth day of July — in the Year of our Lord one thousand eight hundred and eight Before me **Nicholas Diehl, junr.** Notary Public for the Commonwealth of Pennsylvania, by lawful authority duly commissioned and sworn, residing in the city of Philadelphia in the said Commonwealth, and by law authorized to administer oaths and affirmations, Personally appeared John Coulter Part owner of the Brig Niagara of Philada. together with Stephen Russell part owner & Master and Joseph Barker Mate of said Brig

Who being duly Sworn according to law on their solemn Oaths did declare and say, that the said Brig hath not, to the best of their Knowledge & Belief, during her voyage from Philadelphia to Havana & back to Philadelphia, for which voyage Permission hath lately been granted, either directly or indirectly been employed in any Act contrary to the tenor of the Bond executed under the said Permission. —

John Coulter
Stephen Russell
Joseph Barker

Sworn Before me
Nichs. Diehl
Notary Public

Bonded Voyage, Oath of Compliance: *The owner and master of the Brig* Niagara *obtained this notary document, within which they made oath that their vessel did not violate the articles of her Bond, during a voyage from Philadelphia to Havana and back. After acceptance of this document by the Collector at Philadelphia, the Bond would be cancelled. July 25, 1808.*

Early documents were handwritten, with the printed format appearing by the nineteenth century. Usually a one-page document, no standard size, although an approximate measurement of 8 1/2" x 13" was common. The words "Charter Party" often appear prominently in the beginning statement. Occasional small engravings may appear, and the printed name and address of the agent or broker executing the document can sometimes be found near the top.

A Charter Party is a written contract by which the owners or master lets the whole or part of their ship to a merchant for the transportation of goods on a particular voyage. The sum agreed upon to hire the vessel is referred to as the "freight." The document settles the terms upon which the cargo is to be carried. The master or owners usually bind themselves, the ship, tackle and furniture, that the cargo will be delivered (danger of the seas excepted) in good condition, to the place of discharge. They also pledge to sufficiently outfit the ship to properly perform the voyage, and to safely stow the cargo. The merchant or freighter, on his part, promises to comply with the payment for freight upon delivery of his goods, to load and unload in a given amount of time, and to allow so much for demurrage for delays beyond that time. Both parties agree to penalties for non-performance of their respective obligations. Charter Partys are common items in maritime collections, and are valuable research sources for the study of shipping conditions and procedures.

Sold by Bowne & Co 149 Pearl Street, cor Beaver st.

THIS CHARTER PARTY, made and concluded upon in the city of **NEW-YORK**, the *Tenth* day of *November* in the year one thousand eight hundred and forty-*Seven*

Between *Peter Clinton of New York owner*

of the *Brig Tom Paine* of *New York* of the burthen of *One hundred & Ninety eight* — tons or thereabouts, register measurement, now lying in the harbour of New-York, of the first part, and *Charles P Williams*

of Stonington Connecticut Merchant

of the second part, **Witnesseth,** that the said part y of the first part, for and in consideration of the covenants and agreements hereinafter mentioned, to be kept and performed by the said party of the second part, do es covenant and agree on the freighting and chartering of the said vessel unto the said part y of the second part, for a voyage from ~~Ship~~ *The Port of Bucksville South Carolina to the Ports of Mystic and Stonington, Connecticut*

on the terms following, that is to say :

FIRST :—The said part y of the first part, do es engage that the said vessel in and during the said voyage shall be kept tight, staunch, well fitted, tackled, and provided with every requisite, and with men and provisions necessary for such a voyage.

SECOND :—The said part y of the first part, do es further engage that the whole of said vessel (with the exception of the cabin, ████████ and the necessary room for the accommodation of the crew, and the stowage of the sails, cables and provisions,) shall be at the sole use and disposal of the said party of the second part during the voyage aforesaid ; and that no goods or merchandise whatever shall be laden on board, otherwise than from the said party of the second part, or *his* agent, without *his* consent, on pain of forfeiture of the amount of freight agreed upon for the same.

THIRD :—The said part y of the first, do es further engage to take and receive on board the said vessel, during the aforesaid voyage, all such lawful goods and merchandise as the said party of the second part or agents may think proper to ship.

This is the first page of a four-page Charter Party for a coasting voyage from South Carolina to Connecticut, 10 November 1847.

This Charter-Party of Affreightment,

indented, made and fully concluded upon this *Fourteenth* day of *October*
in the year of our LORD one thousand eight hundred and *Eleven* _____ between
William Starrett, John Creighton, James Creighton, Miles Cobb
John Tobey and Eben' Stone

Owners of the good *Schooner America* of the burthen of *One hundred*
Twenty Six tons, or thereabouts, now lying in the harbour of *Thomaston*
whereof *John Tobey* _____ is at present master, on the one part, and
Orris Paine of Savannah in State of Georgia as principal
and John Paine of Thomaston as Surety
on the other part,

Witnesseth, That the said *William John James Miles John & Eben'*
for the consideration hereafter mentioned, ha *ve* letten to freight *or charter* the aforesaid
Schooner with the appurtenances to her belonging, for a voyage to be made by the said
Orris Paine with the said Schooner from Thomaston to any Port or Ports
within the limits of the United States, and from any Port or Ports in
the United States to the West Indias and back so that she may return
to Thomaston within Eight months or thereabouts _____
where she is to be discharged (the danger
of the seas excepted): And the said *William John James Miles John & Eben'*
do by these presents covenant and agree with the said *Orris*
in manner following, *That is to say,* That the said *Schooner*
in and during the voyage aforesaid, shall be tight, staunch and strong, and sufficiently tackled and appa-
relled with all things necessary for such a vessel and voyage ; and that it shall and may be lawful for
the said *Orris Paine or his*
agents or factors, as well at *Thomaston* as at *elsewhere*
to load and put on board the said *Schooner* _____ loading of such goods
and merchandize as they shall think proper, contraband goods excepted.

IN Consideration whereof, the said *Orris Paine*
do *they* by these presents agree with the said *William John James Miles John & Eben'*
well and truly to pay, or cause to be paid, unto *them* in full for the freight or hire of said
Schooner and appurtenances, the sum of *One dollar & fifty Cents per Ton per*
Month while she is employ'd in the Continent Coasting trade and two dollars
per Ton per month for the time she is on the West India Business
and so in proportion for a less time, as the said *Schooner* shall be continued in the aforesaid
service, in *Thirty* days after her return to *Thomaston & is discharged* And the said
Orris Paine do *th* agree to pay the charge
of victualling and manning said *Schooner* and the _____ port charges
and pilotage during said voyage, and to deliver said *Schooner* _____ on her return to
Thomaston _____ to the owners aforesaid or *their* order.

It is understood by the parties that two third of the amount of the
charter that may be due in five months from the date hereof is to be
paid by the said Orris Paine to the owners beforementioned in
all the month of march next and in case the United States should be
War with any foreign nation within the time mentioned for the em-
ploy of said Schooner, the said Orris Paine is to have liberty to return
the said Schooner to the owners aforesaid, paying for the time untill
her return

And to the true and faithful performance of all and singular the covenants, payments and agreements
aforementioned, each of the parties aforenamed binds and obliges himself, his executors and administrators, in the penal sum of *One thousand Dollars* _____
firmly by these presents. In witness whereof, the parties aforesaid have hereunto interchangeably set
their hands and seals the day and year aforewritten.

Signed, sealed and delivered
in presence of us,

W'm Fale
Josiah Reith
Adam Levensaler

Orris Paine
John Paine
William Starrett
James Creighton
Miles Cobb
John Tobey
Eben' Stone

A charter agreement for a voyage to the West Indies, 14 October 1811. Although many
Charter Partys were handwritten at this time, this one-page printed format was not uncommon.

CLASSIFICATION CERTIFICATE

Printed document on paper, approximately 8" x 14". "American Lloyds Register Of Shipping" is printed across the top, and "American Lloyd's" is found within a decorative engraving along the left-hand margin. An engraved eagle also appears, as do American Lloyd's stamps. The Certificate usually displays the signature of the organization's secretary and the port's surveyor.

This Certificate was issued to the shipowner by Lloyd's after a vessel had been surveyed, and was a primary document when the vessel was to be insured. After its establishment in 1857, American Lloyds provided various requirements and levels of classification. Generally speaking, the better a ship's construction and the better the materials used in it, the higher classification rating it would receive. An A1 rating was first class, A1-1/2 second class, A2 third class, A2-1/2 fourth class, and A3 was fifth class. These classes translated into what kind of cargo could be carried. Consequently, first and second class vessels could obtain insurance to transport perishable cargoes on long voyages, while the succeedingly lower classifications indicated less well built, and often older, vessels confined to carrying more durable cargo along shorter distances. Lloyd's would carry the vessel's classification in their *Register*, and indicated that all vessels must be resurveyed "at least once every two years" in order to maintain or revise their classification. (See also Survey Certificate described under Marine Insurance).

AMERICAN LLOYD'S REGISTER OF SHIPPING.

ESTABLISHED 1857.

Committee of Direction—35 Wall St., New York.

Certificate of Classification.

The undersigned Surveyor for the Port of *New York* and vicinity, certifies herewith, that the *Ship Germania of New York* *996* tons, built at *Portsmouth N.H.* in the year *1850* has been duly surveyed by the Surveyor of this Society, and found in a good and efficient state, and fit to carry dry and perishable goods. *On long voyages*

The said vessel will be entered in the American Lloyd's books, and classed A 1½ *Three* years from date of *Survey* and a further continuation of character will be applied in terms of the standard rules, if found sound and staunch, which must be proved at the end of the aforesaid period, and by periodical surveys,—at least one every two years.

In case of vessel being stranded, with damage, must be submitted to a new survey, in order to preserve her class.

Noted Nov '61. Opened forms found in good Condition Ship in general good order

Delivered *by authority,* at *New York Oct 5* 186 *3*

John L Taylor Secretary.

John F.H. King

This Classification Certificate was obtained at the Port of New York by the ship Germania. *The A1-* ½ *rating indicates that the vessel is "fit to carry dry and perishable goods on long voyages." Document was issued by the Port's surveyor.*

CLEARANCE CERTIFICATE

Printed document of various sizes and formats, bearing the signatures of one or more customs officials, i.e. collector, deputy collector, and naval officer. Many display the name of the district and/or port of clearance as a heading. "Clearance" or "General Clearance" is often found, as is the statement, "hath entered and cleared his said vessel according to law". A typical form indicates the names of the vessel and master, registered tonnage, guns mounted (if any), number of crew members, country in which the vessel was built, and the destination of that particular voyage. A general description of the cargo might be included, and the date of issue is usually found near the bottom of this one-page document. Some examples may contain small engravings or have relevant information printed on the backside. Customs stamps or seals are often present.

Any vessel that departed for a foreign port without obtaining a Clearance Certificate was subject to a heavy fine. To obtain clearance papers the master would present a Manifest to the customs collector and swear to the accuracy of the information contained in the papers. Vessels licensed for coastwise trade were not required to formally enter and clear if they were proceeding to another domestic port. However, they had to produce Manifests, or duplicate Manifests if their cargo included foreign goods, before they received permission to proceed. Beginning in 1803 American vessels arriving in foreign ports were required to deliver their papers to the U.S. Consul at that port within 48 hours, or pay a fine that could range from $50.00 to $5,000. The Consul would issue the master a receipt for the papers. Upon leaving, the master obtained a Clearance Certificate from the port authorities. He then took it to the U.S. Consul, who returned the ship's papers, authorizing the vessel to continue its voyage.

I *Abijah Pardee* ——— Master of the *Sloop Resolution*

do solemnly swear to the truth of the annexed *Manifest*, and that to the best of my knowledge and belief, all the Goods, Wares, and Merchandize, of foreign growth or manufacture, therein contained, were legally imported, and the duties thereon paid or secured.

SO HELP ME GOD.

Sworn to 6 day
of *Dec* 1813.

Sam. B. Marshall Collector.

Abijah Pardee

DISTRICT OF NEW-HAVEN.——PORT OF NEW-HAVEN.

Abijah Pardee ——— Master of the *Sloop Resolution* of *New Haven* ——having sworn as the Law directs to the annexed *Manifest*, consisting of *Three* ——— Articles of Entry, and delivered Duplicate thereof, permission is hereby granted to the said *Sloop* to proceed to the port of *New York* in the State of *New York*

Given under my hand, this —6— day of *Decem* 1813.

Sam. B. Marshall Collector.

Clearance Certificate issued at New Haven, Connecticut, *for a coastwise passage to New York, 6 December 1813.*

CLEARANCE CERTIFICATE

PORT OF NEW-YORK.

THESE ARE TO CERTIFY all whom it doth concern,

That *James P. Sheffield* Master,

or Commander of the *Brig Bogota*

burthen *154 1/2* Tons, or

thereabouts, mounted with *Two* Guns, navigated

with *Nine* Men *American* built,

and bound for *Gibraltar*

having on board *Flour, Rice Tobacco, Cocoa & and Stores*

hath here entered and cleared his said vessel according to law.

GIVEN under our hands and seals at the Custom House of New-York, this *31st* day of *March* one thousand eight hundred and twenty *eight* and in the *52d* year of the Independence of the United States of America.

[GENERAL CLEARANCE.]

Sam'l L. Gardiner
COLLECTOR.

David Lyon
NAVAL OFFICER.

Clearance Certificate issued at New York for a foreign voyage, 31 March 1828.

CERTIFICATE OF CLEARANCE,

HAWAIIAN ISLANDS.

Port of Honolulu, *Nov. 21st* 1859

This is to certify, that the *Oscar* of which

Sanders is Master, bound for *a cruise*

is at liberty to proceed on her voyage.

J. V. Eagles
Collector.

Bark Oscar

To Collector General of Customs   Dr

To Buoys,	2
To Pilotage in, 15 feet, out, 15 feet,	30
To Certificate of Clearance,	1
To Stamps and Blanks,	2
Fees	2 50
	39 50

Received Payment,

J. V. Eagles
Collector

Honolulu, Nov. 21st 1859.

Clearance issued at Honolulu *for a whaling voyage, 21 November 1859.*

COASTING PERMIT

> (COASTING PERMIT.)
>
> Port of Great Egg Harbour.
>
> *Isaac Willitts* — Master of the *Sloop Polly & Nancy*
> of *Gt Egg Harbour* measuring
> 58 75/95 Tons, is hereby authorised to proceed with the said *Sloop*
> and cargo consisting of *Lumber* and classed in
> *two* articles of Entry, as specified in the manifest annexed,
> to the Port of *Philadelphia* in *Philadelphia* District,
> the said Master having complied with the "*Act for enrolling and licensing ships or*
> "*vessels to be employed in the coasting trade and fisheries and for regulating the same.*"
> WITNESS my hand at the Custom House, *April the 8* 1809.
>
> *John W Bunner &c*
>
> *Embargo Bond given*

The Coasting Permit was a customs document required to be carried by shipmasters of vessels transporting certain previously imported goods from one U.S. port to another. They were generally small, undecorated forms, and carried the signature of the issuing customs official. Coasting Permits were authorized by 1790 and 1793 legislation that dealt with licensing and enrollment of American vessels, but these permits were valid for one voyage only, and were used in addition to these other documents.

The master of a ship carrying certain imported goods, such as wine, sugar, and tea (or distilled spirits manufactured in the U.S.) made duplicate Manifests of all the vessel's cargo. He then delivered them to the collector and swore that, to the best of his knowledge, the goods had been legally imported and all appropriate duties paid. The collector would then certify the oath on the Manifests, and return one to the master along with the Coasting Permit attached, which described the cargo and authorized him to proceed on his intended voyage. Coasting Permits are representative of the many documents and forms used by the United States during the early years of the nineteenth century to protect American markets from illegal importation and transportation of foreign goods.

The United States Consular Service was established on 14 April 1792, as a branch of the State Department, to promote American commerce and protect American interests abroad. President George Washington, in his address to the first Congress, stated that "the patronage of our Commerce, of our merchants and seamen, called for the appointment of consuls in foreign countries." Consular officers were public officials appointed by the government, residing in foreign lands to perform administrative and judicial functions for the benefit of American citizens residing there. A Consul was usually assigned to every major port. Occasionally some large or exceptionally active ports might also have a Deputy Consul. Consular Agents served smaller ports or islands that might fall within a larger district. Commercial Agents were often equal in rank to a Consul, but were not appointed by the President. Instead they were commissioned by the State Department as "executive agents sent abroad for the promotion and advancement of commercial interests." These Commercial Agents were frequently businessmen with their own interests at the ports where they were assigned. They were often found in places where formal diplomatic relations between that nation and the United States were not established or required. In 1856 there were approximately 200 Consuls, 85 Consular Agents, and 19 Commercial Agents employed by the State Department at ports throughout the world. The selection of certificates included here, in addition to some others found elsewhere in this book, should provide a useful source for understanding the role played by the Consular Service in the conduct of American shipping in foreign lands.

I JAMES MAURY,

CONSUL of the *United States of America*,

For the Port of LIVERPOOL,

And for the Ports of GREAT BRITAIN *nearer thereto than to any other*
AMERICAN CONSULATE,

Do Certify and Make Known to whom thefe Prefents
fhall come, That

The Vessel called the Juno of Bristol John Kendrick Master in consequence of additions since her arrival at this Port is now Armed with Ten Carriage Guns

*...*n from under my Hand, and Seal of Office, at
Liverpool, *the* 3ᵈ Day of *November*
and Year One Thousand Eight Hundred and One

James Maury

Thos. Bigland

This generic Consular Certificate *was used to indicate that the ship* Juno *of Bristol, Rhode Island, received 10 carriage guns at the Port of Liverpool in 1801. Whether for protection or to privateer against the French,* Juno *was armed with the knowledge and consent of the United States government. Certificate contains the signature of the U.S. Consul and the customary consular seal.*

CONSULATE OF THE UNITED STATES OF AMERICA.

THESE are to certify, that I have this day delivered the Register of the *Brig Steele*

of *Phrrass* to *Fank Watty* the

Master thereof, and have received from him the sum of Four Dollars according to law, for the undermentioned

services :

Deposit and delivery of Ship's Papers and Certificates, – – – – – – $ 4 00.

GIVEN under my hand, at Pictou, and the Seal of the Agency of the said Consulate,

at Halifax, this *29* day of *Augt.* A. D. 183 *4*

and the 61st year of the Independance of the said United States.

Consular agent

Certificate of Delivery of Ship's Papers, *indicating that the ship's papers have been returned to the master of an American vessel at a foreign port. This usually plain, printed document varied in size and style, but displayed the consular seal, and often stated the charge for deposit and delivery of the papers. Certificates like this are fairly common in collections of maritime manuscripts.*

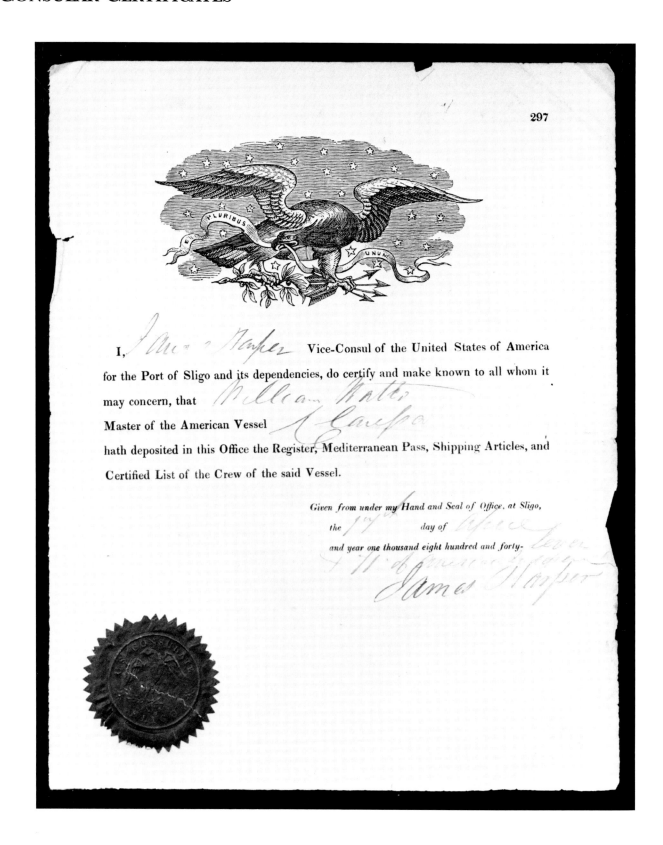

297

I, *James Harper* Vice-Consul of the United States of America for the Port of Sligo and its dependencies, do certify and make known to all whom it may concern, that *William Watts* Master of the American Vessel *Europa* hath deposited in this Office the Register, Mediterranean Pass, Shipping Articles, and Certified List of the Crew of the said Vessel.

Given from under my Hand and Seal of Office, at Sligo, the *first* day of *April* and year one thousand eight hundred and forty-*seven*

James Harper

This Certificate of Deposit for Ship's Papers was *given to masters of American vessels, indicating receipt of the required ship's papers. The papers were held by the Consul until the vessel had cleared and was ready to depart. This printed form varied in size and style, but often included Consular seal and signature of the official issuing the document. This document contains the signature of a Vice Consul, acting in a temporary capacity during the absence of a Consul.*

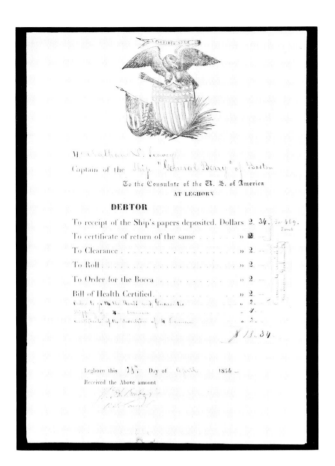

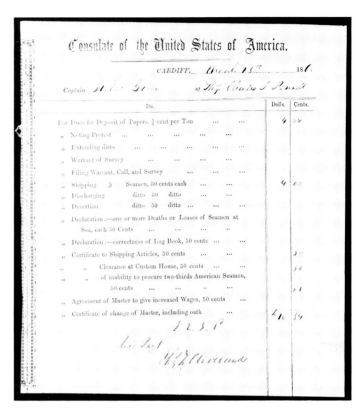

Part of a ship's expenses in foreign ports *was for particular services provided by the resident consular authority. Before departure, a bill for these services was presented to the master. The consular official's signature acknowledged receipt of payment and the date received. The examples illustrated above show the variety of forms, services, and charges at various ports during the late 1850s. Also, each consular officer was required at this time to number all receipts given by him, in order of their date, but only the Honolulu document carries this number, i.e. #217.*

CONTRIBUTION CERTIFICATE

Printed certificate, approximately 6 1/2" x 4". *Many examples have engraved borders with decorative scenes of a brig along a coastline located in the center of the certificate. Scrolls to the right and left provided space to record the sum contributed and the equivalent number of shares accorded, usually at ten cents per share. Contains the signature of the Treasurer for the American Board of Commissioners for Foreign Missions, located in Boston.*

In 1856, the Hawaiian Board of the Hawaiian Evangelical Association asked the American Board of Commissioners for Foreign Missions to help them raise funds for a vessel that would aid mission work in Hawaii, Micronesia, and the Marquesa Islands. Traffic between the islands was irregular, and missions often had difficulty procuring basic supplies. In August 1856, the American Board appealed to children in the United States to help purchase a missionary packet by buying ten-cent shares of ownership. In return, the children received Certificates of Contribution. One-hundred twenty thousand Americans became stockholders, and by year's end the Morning Star, *a hermaphrodite brig, had been built in Chelsea, Massachusetts, at a cost of $18,351.00. Launched in Boston, the* Morning Star *arrived at Honolulu in April, 1857 and continued to sail between South Pacific missions until she was sold in 1866. Five more* Morning Stars *succeeded her, all of which were funded by similar appeals.*

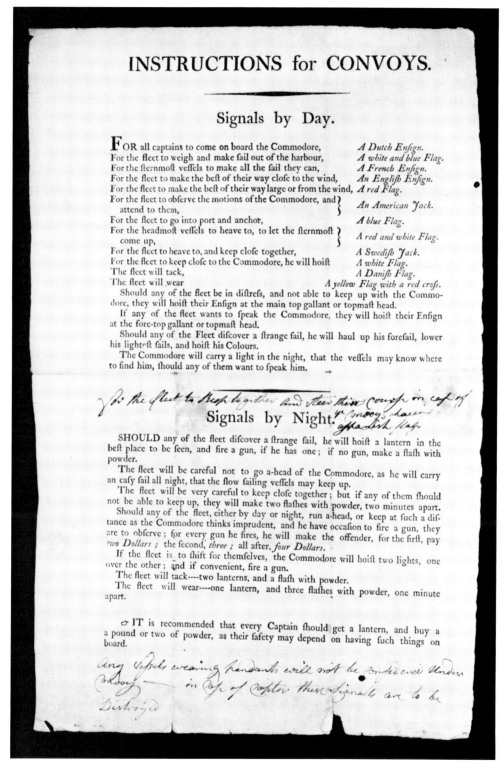

INSTRUCTIONS for CONVOYS.

Signals by Day.

FOR all captains to come on board the Commodore,	*A Dutch Enfign.*
For the fleet to weigh and make fail out of the harbour,	*A white and blue Flag.*
For the fternmoft veffels to make all the fail they can,	*A French Enfign.*
For the fleet to make the beft of their way clofe to the wind,	*An Englifh Enfign.*
For the fleet to make the beft of their way large or from the wind,	*A red Flag.*
For the fleet to obferve the motions of the Commodore, and attend to them,	*An American Jack.*
For the fleet to go into port and anchor,	*A blue Flag.*
For the headmoft veffels to heave to, to let the fternmoft come up,	*A red and white Flag.*
For the fleet to heave to, and keep clofe together,	*A Swedifh Jack.*
For the fleet to keep clofe to the Commodore, he will hoift	*A white Flag.*
The fleet will tack,	*A Danifh Flag.*
The fleet will wear	*A yellow Flag with a red crofs.*

Should any of the fleet be in diftrefs, and not able to keep up with the Commodore, they will hoift their Enfign at the main top gallant or topmaft head.

If any of the fleet wants to fpeak the Commodore, they will hoift their Enfign at the fore-top gallant or topmaft head.

Should any of the Fleet difcover a ftrange fail, he will haul up his forefail, lower his lighteft fails, and hoift his Colours.

The Commodore will carry a light in the night, that the veffels may know where to find him, fhould any of them want to fpeak him.

[handwritten:] for the fleet to keep together and steer their course in case of Convoys chase ... Spanish flag

Signals by Night.

SHOULD any of the fleet difcover a ftrange fail, he will hoift a lantern in the beft place to be feen, and fire a gun, if he has one; if no gun, make a flafh with powder.

The fleet will be careful not to go a-head of the Commodore, as he will carry an eafy fail all night, that the flow failing veffels may keep up.

The fleet will be very careful to keep clofe together; but if any of them fhould not be able to keep up, they will make two flafhes with powder, two minutes apart.

Should any of the fleet, either by day or night, run a-head, or keep at fuch a diftance as the Commodore thinks imprudent, and he have occafion to fire a gun, they are to obferve; for every gun he fires, he will make the offender, for the firft, pay *two Dollars*; the fecond, *three*; all after, *four Dollars.*

If the fleet is to fhift for themfelves, the Commodore will hoift two lights, one over the other; and if convenient, fire a gun.

The fleet will tack----two lanterns, and a flafh with powder.

The fleet will wear----one lantern, and three flafhes with powder, one minute apart.

☞ IT is recommended that every Captain fhould get a lantern, and buy a pound or two of powder, as their fafety may depend on having fuch things on board.

[handwritten:] Any Vessels wearing pendants will not be confidered under Convoy — in case of capture their Signals are to be Destroyed

***Convoy Instructions were issued by** the protecting naval force, and outlined procedures and conduct required of every vessel in the convoy. The example above was a British document given to an American merchant vessel, sailing as a neutral under British protection, ca. 1800. Instructions were usually printed, and often varied in detail and composition. The signature of the convoy commander and the name of the vessel or master receiving the instructions might appear on the document as well as illustrations – sometimes in color – of the flag or lantern codes used during the voyage. These documents might be found in collections of American maritime manuscripts from the colonial and early national periods, when our interests on the high seas were much less secure.*

CREW LIST

A printed document, varying in size and format. Contains the names and descriptions of every member of a ship's company. Across the top was printed "A List of the Company," "List of Persons," or perhaps "Role d'Equipage," the French term. The master's name, ship's name, destination, and tonnage was often found on the upper portion of the document, where some examples displayed engraved eagles, etc. The body of the Crew List consisted of columns containing names, ages, places of birth and residence, and other descriptive information, such as complexion and crew status. The kinds of information requested varied from one document to another. Some examples also include a column for witnesses' signatures. Depending upon the immediate use of the document, it could contain the signatures of the shipmaster, the customs collector, and consular official, or a combination thereof. Some examples were certified not only with authorized signatures, but by various stamps and seals as well.

The Act of 28 February 1803 contained the first legal mention and requirements for keeping a Crew List as part of the ship's papers. Before a vessel could depart on a foreign voyage, the master had to deliver a list of the crew, verified by his oath, to the customs collector at that port. The collector then supplied the master with a certified copy of the list, copied in a uniform hand, along with a Clearance Certificate, at which time the master entered into a four-hundred-dollar bond to exhibit the Crew List to the first boarding officer he encountered upon his return to a U.S. port. There he was required to produce the persons named and described in the Crew List, and to give account for any crew members who were not present. Notes certifying sickness, discharge or desertion, usually signed by a consular official, were often included with the original list in order to prove that individuals not present were legally accounted for. Crew Lists of various kinds are commonly found in maritime collections. In addition to the formal document described here, a list of crew members usually appears on the Articles of Agreement, and such lists are often written in ships' logbooks or journals.

A List of the Company of the *Schooner Sally*
James Day Master, 90 89/95 Tons, bound to *Barbadoes*
New-London, *June 13* 18*01*

Men's names.	Quality.	Places of birth.	Places of residence.	Age.	Complexion.
James Day	Master	Sheffield	New London	29	Light
Park Allyn	Mate	Groton	Groton	45	Light
Moses Pendleton	Seaman	Stonington	Stonington	26	Dark
James Peckham	Seaman	Stonington	Stonington	21	Light
Sam'l Wood	Seaman	New London	New London	19	Light
Bradford Phillips	Seaman	Groton	Groton	19	Light
Joseph Hewit	Cook	New London	New London	17	Light
B. Marks	Seaman	Orleans	New York	26	Negro

I solemnly swear that the foregoing list contains the names of the crew of said vessel, together with the places of their birth and residence, as far as I am able to ascertain them. *So help me God.*

Master.

James Day

District and port of NEW-LONDON, *13 June*   18*01*
The foregoing is a true copy of the original.
Certified by
A. Woodward, jno.   Collector.

Official Crew List *typical of those used during the early nineteenth century. Note the uniform hand of crew members' data, the master's oath, and collector's certification.*

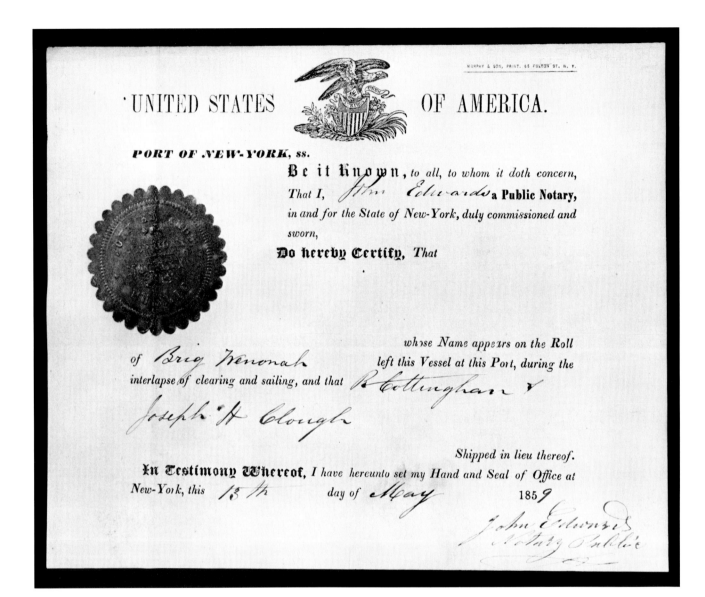

MURPHY & SON, PRINT. 65 FULTON ST. N. Y.

UNITED STATES OF AMERICA.

PORT OF NEW-YORK, ss.

Be it Known, to all, to whom it doth concern, That I, *John Edwards* a Public Notary, in and for the State of New-York, duly commissioned and sworn,

Do hereby Certify, That

of *Brig Wenonah*

whose Name appears on the Roll left this Vessel at this Port, during the interlapse of clearing and sailing, and that *R. Cottingham & Joseph H. Clough*

Shipped in lieu thereof.

In Testimony Whereof, I have hereunto set my Hand and Seal of Office at New-York, this *15th* day of *May* 185*9*

John Edwards
Notary Public

Crew List Certificate of Change: If a ship had already obtained a clearance from the customs collector or consular official at a port, and a change in the composition of the crew was made, some official documentation of the change was required. A Certificate of Change could be obtained quickly from a notary public, thus authenticating the alteration and avoiding problems at the next port. The document included the names of crew members who left or boarded the vessel before sailing, the vessel's name, and the notary's signature and official seal.

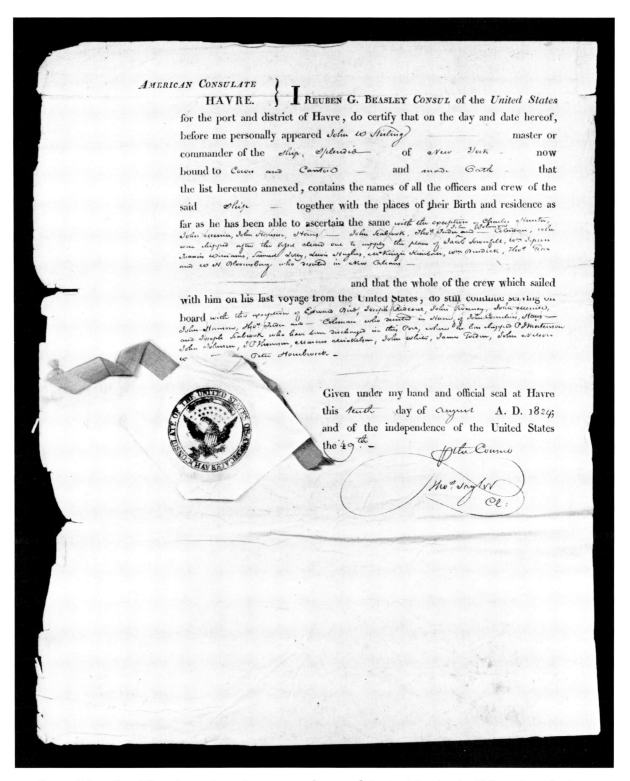

AMERICAN CONSULATE

HAVRE. I REUBEN G. BEASLEY CONSUL of the United States for the port and district of Havre, do certify that on the day and date hereof, before me personally appeared *John W. Stirling* master or commander of the *Ship, Splendid* of *New York* now bound to *Cowes and Canton* and *made Oath* that the list hereunto annexed, contains the names of all the officers and crew of the said *Ship* together with the places of their Birth and residence as far as he has been able to ascertain the same *with the exception of Charles S. Hunter, John Luenix, John Hawson, Harry — John Seabrook, Thos Foster and John Wilmington Coleman, who were shipped after the Vessel cleared one to supply the place of Isaac Townfield, Wm Iprion Francis Williams, Samuel Luley, Lewis Hughes, McKinzie Kimber, Wm Brudick, Thos For and W N Bloomsbury who resided in New Orleans*

and that the whole of the crew which sailed with him on his last voyage from the United States, do still continue serving on board *with the exception of Edward Bird, Joseph Ridcour, John Rooney, John Luenix, John Hawson, Thos Foster and — Coleman who resided in Havre, of Ivan Cornelius, Harry — and Joseph Seabrook who have been discharged in this Port, where he has shipped O J Masterson John Johnson, J T Thomson, Marcus Crickelow, John White, James Foster, John Nelson W — Peter Hombwick —*

Given under my hand and official seal at Havre this *tenth* day of *August* A. D. 1824; and of the independence of the United States the 49 *th* —

Pro Consul
Thos Saylor
Cl:

Crew List Certification: *Any time a vessel entered port, either in the U.S. or in a foreign country where there was a consulate, the master was required to exhibit the Crew List to a customs or consular official. The officer would then fill out a Crew List Certification, stating that the boarding officer had compared the list and other relevant ship's papers to the actual crew members. These documents varied in format, but necessarily included the vessel's name and home port, the master's name, and the names of any seamen who appeared on the crew list, but who had deserted or been discharged. When properly executed, the certification carried the Collector's or Consul's signature, and official stamps and seals.*

KNOW all Men by thefe Prefents, that we *Jos. Whitney* _____ of *Providence in the State of Rhode Ifland &c.* _____ Mafter or Commander of the *Ship Palmyra,* _____ now lying in the Diftrict of Providence, and *Jos. T. Martin of faid Providence, Merchant,* _____ are held and firmly bound unto the United States of America, in the full and juft fum of Four Hundred Dollars, money of the United States; to which payment, well and truly to be made, we bind ourfelves jointly and feverally, our joint and feveral heirs, executors and adminiftrators, firmly by thefe prefents. Sealed with our feals, and dated this *Fifteenth* _____ day of *November* One Thoufand Eight Hundred and *Six.*

WHEREAS the above bounden *Jos. Whitney* _____ hath delivered to the Collector of the Cuftoms for the Diftrict of Providence, in the State of Rhode-Ifland, &c. a verified lift containing, as far as he can afcertain them, the names, places of birth, refidence and defcription of the perfons who compofe the company of the faid *Ship Palmyra,* now lying in the faid diftrict, of which he is at prefent Mafter or Commander; of which lift the faid Collector has delivered to the faid Mafter a certified copy: NOW THE CONDITION of this obligation is fuch that if the faid *Whitney* _____ fhall exhibit the aforefaid certified copy of the lift to the firft boarding officer, at the firft port in the United States at which fhe fhall arrive on his return thereto, and then and there alfo produce the perfons named therein to the faid boarding officer, except any of the perfons contained in the faid lift, who may be difcharged in a foreign country, with the confent of the conful, vice-conful, commercial agent or vice-commercial agent, there refiding, fignified in writing under his hand and official feal, to be produced to the Collector of the diftrict within which he may arrive as aforefaid, with the other perfons compofing the crew as aforefaid, or who may have died or abfconded, or who may have been forcibly impreffed into other fervice, of which fatisfactory proof fhall be then alfo exhibited to the faid laft mentioned Collector, then and in fuch cafe the above obligation fhall be void and of no effect, otherwife it fhall abide and remain in full force and virtue.

Sealed and delivered
in prefence of
Geo. Olney

Joseph Whitney

Joseph P Martin

***Crew List Bond:** A bond in the amount of $400.00 signed by the shipmaster and others, within which he agrees to comply with all legal obligations regarding the Crew List during the upcoming voyage. (Courtesy of Rhode Island Historical Society.)*

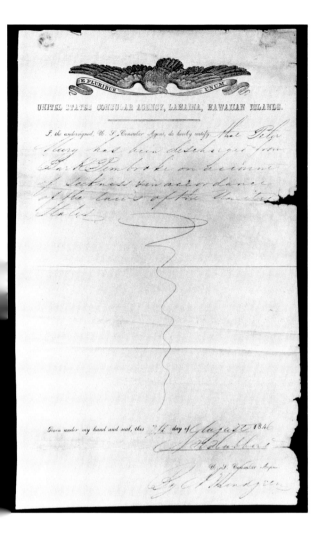

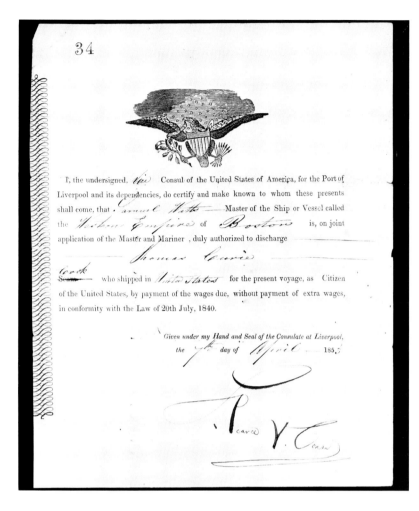

Discharge Certificates *were used to record the discharge of crew members from American vessels at foreign ports. These documents varied in size and format. However, they usually included the name or names of seamen being discharged, the vessel's name and home port, the master's name, and the reason for discharge. The U.S. Consul or other qualified official signed and sealed the document. It was given to the shipmaster who placed it with the Crew List as proof of the alteration in the composition of the crew. Individual discharge receipts were also given to each person discharged.*

CONSULATE OF THE UNITED STATES OF AMERICA, LIVERPOOL.

I, _Samuel Pearce Vice_ Consul of the United States of America for Liverpool and the Dependencies thereof, do certify that the Seamen or Mariners hereinafter described have been Shipped at this Port, to proceed on a voyage to _the United States_ on board of the _Ship Ariel_ of _Bath_ as appears by the declaration of _J.? A? Abed_ Master of said _Ship_ made before me this day

Names	Of what Country Citizens or Subjects (as alleged.)	Wages ℗ month		Description of Person.			
				Age.	Height.	Complexion.	Hair.
John Blackstock	United States	4		22	5. 9	Light	
James Richardson	do	4		35	5. 5	Dark	
Thomas Scholes	do	4		29	5. 8	Light	
James Walker	do	. 2		24	5. 6	Dark	
Hugh Morris	do	2 10		37	5. 9	Light	
George Williams	do	2 10		39	5. 6	"	
Joseph White	do	2 10		25	5. 7	"	
James Watson	do	2 10		22	5. 7	"	
Alex.ᵈ King	do	2 10		35	5. 8	Dark	
Edward Sykes	do	2 10		23	5. 8	"	
James Jones	do	2 10		20	5. 7	Light	
John Wenn	do	2 10		22	5. 11		
Henry Jones	do	2 10		22	5. 6		
John Curry	do	2 10		22	5. 8		
Geor.ᵍ Taylor	do	2 10		27	5. 6	Dark	
Francis Sullivan	do	2 10		20	5. 7	Light	
George Shaw	do	2 10		21	5. 7	Dark	
William Robertson	do	2 10		32	5. 6	Light	
Horace Pogg	do	2 10		21	5. 7	"	
Henry B??	noproof	5		22	5. 8	"	
John M?Laren	do	. 2		32	5. 9	Dark	
Patk Gunnity		. 2		25	5. 7	"	
Patk M?Gothcok		. 2		23	5. 7	Light	
William Johnson	United States	2 10		39	5. 7		
Jas Daly							

In testimony whereof, I have hereunto set my hand and affixed the Seal of the Consulate of the United States at LIVERPOOL aforesaid, this _11_ day of _April_ in the Year of our Lord One Thousand Eight Hundred and Fifty _three_ and in the Seven _ty Seventh_ Year of the Independence of the said United States.

Sam Pearce
Vice Consul

Consul's Certificate of Crewmen Shipped: *This document contains the names of individuals shipped as crew members aboard the ship* Ariel *by the U.S. Consul at Liverpool. Like the customs service Crew List previously described, the Consul's Certificate also exhibits the uniform hand and other similar information. This copy was given to the shipmaster, who would then produce it, along with the original crew list and other related documents, upon his arrival at the first port of call in the United States.*

DmI.1.1

DISTRICT AND PORT OF NEW-YORK, *March* 183 4

SIR,

The certified Copy of the List containing the names, places of birth, residence, and a description of persons composing the crew of the *Barque Dragon* — of *New Bedford* whereof *Enos Pope* — is Master granted in the District of *New Bedford* on the *thirteenth* day of *September* — has been returned to this office, with a Certificate of the Boarding Officer thereon, stating that the persons produced to him correspond with said List, except where they are otherwise noted.....to wit:

RETURNED, *except* *William Wells, acc.d for by aff.t*

Thomas Boyer acc.d for by Consul.

I am, Sir,

Your most obedient Servant,

SAMUEL SWARTWOUT,

COLLECTOR.

To the Collector of the Customs,
District of *New Bedford.*

Customs Certificate of Crew List Examination: *The Act of 1803 required the master of any ship returning from a foreign voyage to produce all relevant Crew List documents to the boarding officer of the first U.S. port he returned to. The document above, from the Collector at New York to the Collector at New Bedford, reveals that the bark* Dragon *had first arrived in New York and that the certified copy of the Crew List had been inspected with alterations noted.*

CREW LIST

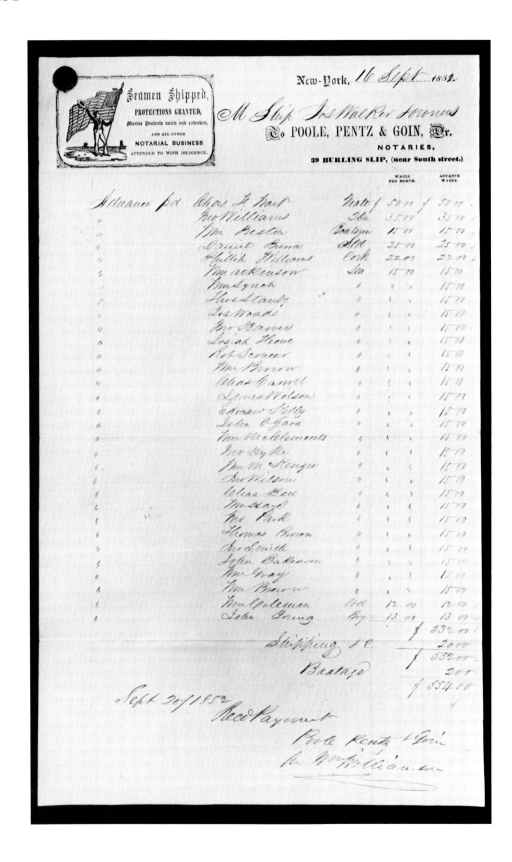

Various kinds of "Crew Lists" can be found in maritime collections. Shown here is a bill from an agent to the shipowners for signing up 31 men. A total of $532.00 was advanced to them, and the agent charged $20.00 plus $2.00 for boating them to the ship.

Following the American Revolution, each state attempted to set up a customs service of its own. However, by 1789 it was apparent that a more consistent and coordinated Federal service was necessary. On 31 July of that year, President Washington signed legislation which established the United States Customs Service. As a branch of the Treasury Department, it became the first fully-formed national agency, and was created primarily to generate much-needed revenue for the new government.

Initially there were 59 customs districts set up in 11 states. Each district employed a customs collector, appointed by the President, and a naval officer. Other officials assisted the collector at the various ports within each district. The larger ports like New York and Boston would employ various numbers of surveyors, weighers, gaugers, inspectors, and revenue-cutter crews, all with specific responsibilities for the conduct of business at the port.

The Customs Service was originally responsible for the collection of duties on imported goods, the registering and licensing of American vessels, the enforcement of all maritime and navigation laws, and the management of regulations governing the entry and clearance of seamen and passengers. While these functions remained, responsibilities were expanded and became more specialized during the nineteenth century. After 1793, regulatory forms for exports as well as imports were required. Between 1798 and 1809, the customs enforced the various embargo and non-intercourse laws, issued regulatory documentation, and initiated libel action against violators. The Marine Hospital, providing care for sick or disabled seamen, was founded in 1798, and the customs officials were delegated to collect hospital fees from vessels arriving at their port. After 1819, customs districts were required to collect the passenger lists of all vessels arriving from foreign ports. Other responsibilities included holding imported goods in bonded warehouses until the duty was paid (1846); keeping official records on the sale of vessels (1850); and regulating steamship commerce and safety.

By 1860, the increasing complexity of regulating maritime commerce had made the customs service a large agency, responsible for nearly one half of the revenue taken in by the Federal government.

What follows is a representative selection of customs forms and certificates issued by port officials, and/or recorded by them as part of their daily activities. Along with related items like bonds, oaths, and receipts, found elsewhere in this book, they can provide the reader with a better understanding of what the customs service did during this period, and just what documents were required for the lawful conduct of maritime business.

Certificate For a Vessel Going to Another District *with Inward Bound Cargo on which Duties have not been paid This is an example of the many kinds of documents used during this period by the customs districts to control the movement of imported goods within the United States, for the purpose of securing all appropriate duties before they entered the private market. In this example the brig* Susan *landed and paid duty on the cargo described at New York. The Certificate, issued through the collector there, indicates that the master has posted a bond in order to take the remainder of his cargo to Hartford.*

No. 332   DISTRICT of *New London*

Office of Inspection for the Port of *New London*

I CERTIFY that it appears from the Report of *John Colton*,
Master of the *brig Caroline*   duly made to this Office, that the
following kinds and quantities of distilled Spirits were imported in said *brig*
from *Montego Bay*   viz.

Marks.	Description of Casks, Vessels and Cases.	Numbers of Casks, Vessels and Cases.	Kind of Spirits.	Quantities in Gallons.
B C	Puncheon	17	Rum	
L R	Ditto	1	do.	
I C	do	9	do.	
I M I	Ditto	7	do.	
		34		

And that it appears from *Permits* granted by the Collector of the Customs for the
District of ———————— which have been by me *inspected*, that the following
quantities of said Spirits have been discharged at this Port,   -   -   -   viz.

Marks.	Description of Casks, Vessels, and Cases.	Numbers of Casks, Vessels and Cases.	Kind of Spirits.	Quantities in Gallons.
			Reshipped for Connecticut River	

Given under my Hand, and Seal of Office, this   day
of   17

Nat Richards   Inspector,

Certificate of Importation and Discharge: *The movement and control of imported spirits, rum, wine, etc., provided an important source of revenue for the new American government. This Certificate, signed by a Inspector at the Port of New London, indicates that 34 puncheons of rum had arrived aboard the brig* Caroline, *but was to be discharged later at a destination along the Connecticut River in 1796.*

Entry of Baggage Permit: *Personal baggage was inspected for dutiable articles. This document, signed by the collector, authorized the inspector to examine the baggage of a Mrs. Robard, arriving from France in November 1810. In this case a marginal notation indicates that the three trunks contained false bottoms which hid dutiable goods.*

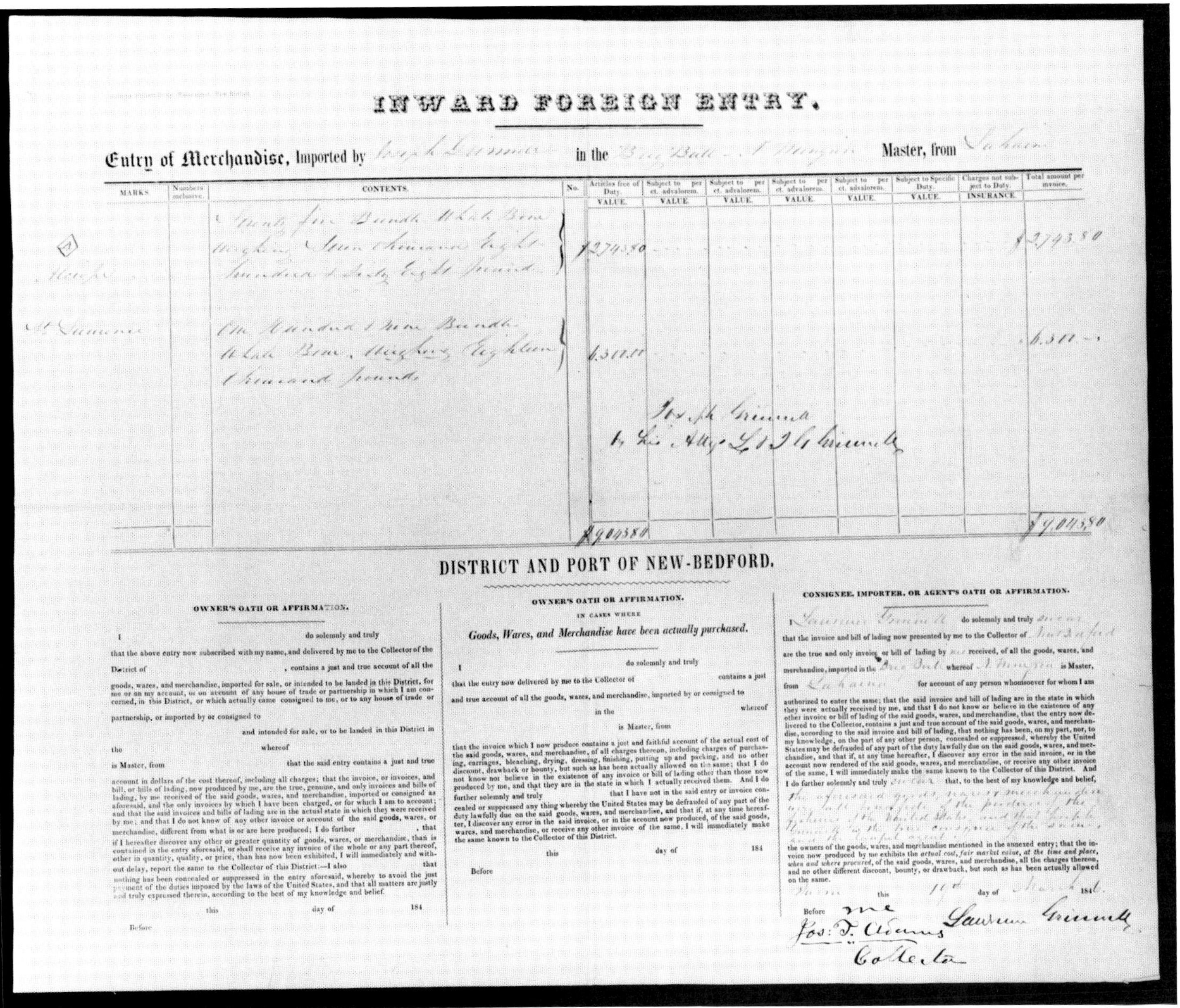

INWARD FOREIGN ENTRY.

Entry of Merchandise, Imported by _Joseph Grinnell_ in the _Bark Bell — N Mangin_ Master, from _Lahaina_

MARKS	Numbers inclusive	CONTENTS	No.	Articles free of Duty. VALUE.	Subject to per ct. advalorem. VALUE.	Subject to per ct. advalorem. VALUE.	Subject to per ct. advalorem. VALUE.	Subject to per ct. advalorem. VALUE.	Subject to Specific Duty. VALUE.	Charges not subject to Duty. INSURANCE.	Total amount per invoice.
⌂		Twenty five Bundle Whale Bone Weighing Seven thousand eight hundred & sixty eight pounds		$2743.80							$2743.80
		One hundred & nine Bundle Whale Bone, Weighing Eighteen thousand pounds		6311.00							6311.00
		Jos. M. Grinnell by his Atty. J. D. Grinnell									
				$9054.80							$9054.80

DISTRICT AND PORT OF NEW-BEDFORD.

OWNER'S OATH OR AFFIRMATION.	OWNER'S OATH OR AFFIRMATION. IN CASES WHERE *Goods, Wares, and Merchandise have been actually purchased.*	CONSIGNEE, IMPORTER, OR AGENT'S OATH OR AFFIRMATION.

(Oath text in printed columns, partially legible)

Before _Jos. F. Adams_ _Lawrence Grinnell_
Collector

Inward Foreign Entry Certificate: *This customs document, in various forms, was issued through the collector whenever imported foreign cargo arrived in his district. It contains a description of the goods, and in addition required an oath from the owner, agent, or consignee, that the items were legally imported, that the manifest was accurate, and that the appropriate duties had been paid. Once the Certificate was completed to the collector's satisfaction, he signed it and the goods were released from the port's authority.*

198 Tons

PORT OF NEW-YORK.
—
TO THE INSPECTORS OF THE PORT.

S Watts Master of the *Brig Clarissa*

from *N Orleans,* having produced to us a certified Manifest of all the

Cargo on board said vessel, consisting of

Pork Hams,
Lard, Molasses, Sugar

Permission is hereby given to land the same.

CUSTOM-HOUSE, *5 Apr* 1842

COLLECTOR.

NAVAL OFFICER.

Permit to Land Cargo: *This customs document, varying in size and form, was almost always signed by the collector and naval officer, and then given to the shipmaster. It indicated that the ship's papers were in order and that, in the case of foreign goods, all relevant duties had been paid. After presenting the Permit to the inspector, the shipmaster could then unload his cargo.*

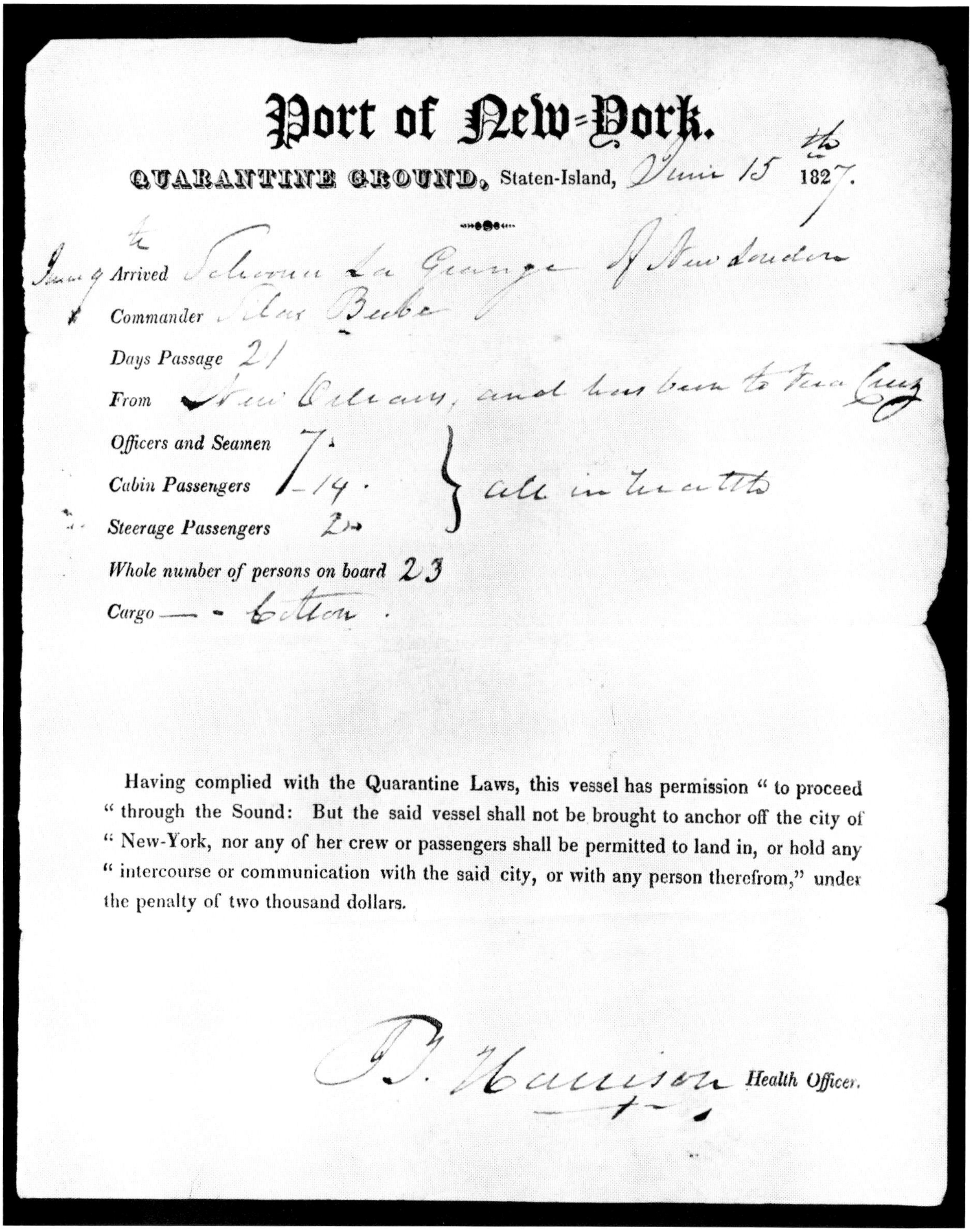

Port of New=York.

QUARANTINE GROUND, Staten-Island, *June 15th 1827.*

Arrived *Schooner La Grange of New London*

Commander *Silas Bube*

Days Passage *21*

From *New Orleans, and has been to Vera Cruz*

Officers and Seamen *7*

Cabin Passengers *14* } *all in health*

Steerage Passengers *2*

Whole number of persons on board *23*

Cargo — *Cotton.*

Having complied with the Quarantine Laws, this vessel has permission " to proceed
" through the Sound: But the said vessel shall not be brought to anchor off the city of
" New-York, nor any of her crew or passengers shall be permitted to land in, or hold any
" intercourse or communication with the said city, or with any person therefrom," under
the penalty of two thousand dollars.

B. Harrison Health Officer.

Permit to Leave Quarantine Ground: *A customs document, issued by the port's Health Officer, indicating that the vessel has complied with the quarantine regulations and that everyone aboard has been pronounced in good health. The vessel was then able to enter port, discharge passengers and cargo, and conduct ship's business. However, in the permit illustrated here, the schooner* La Grange, *from New Orleans, spent six days in quarantine before being cleared only "to proceed through the Sound," but not come ashore in New York, subject to a $2,000 fine.*

CUSTOMS CERTIFICATES AND FORMS

Form of Certificate to be granted by the Store-Keeper, for Merchandize lodged in the Public Store. District of New-York.—Port of New-York, *July 21 — 1808 —* **I Certify** that there has been received into store, from on board the *Sch: President* whereof *Gillet* is master, from the following merchandize, to wit,

One Hundred & Eighty nine Barrels Flour } said to be
One Hundred & Ninety nine Kegs — } Seized.

lodged by *Van Beuren* — inspector, under whose care the said vessel was unladen. *Jonas Addoms*

Certificate of Deposit in the Public Store: *Illegal goods, or items on which duties had not been paid, were discharged from the vessel and put into a warehouse, often called the Public Store. They remained there under the supervision of a customs official (i.e. the store keeper) until such time as the duties were paid by the consignee, or perhaps sold at public auction for the benefit of the government. The receipt illustrated here reveals that a large shipment of flour had been seized and deposited in the Public Store by the inspector.*

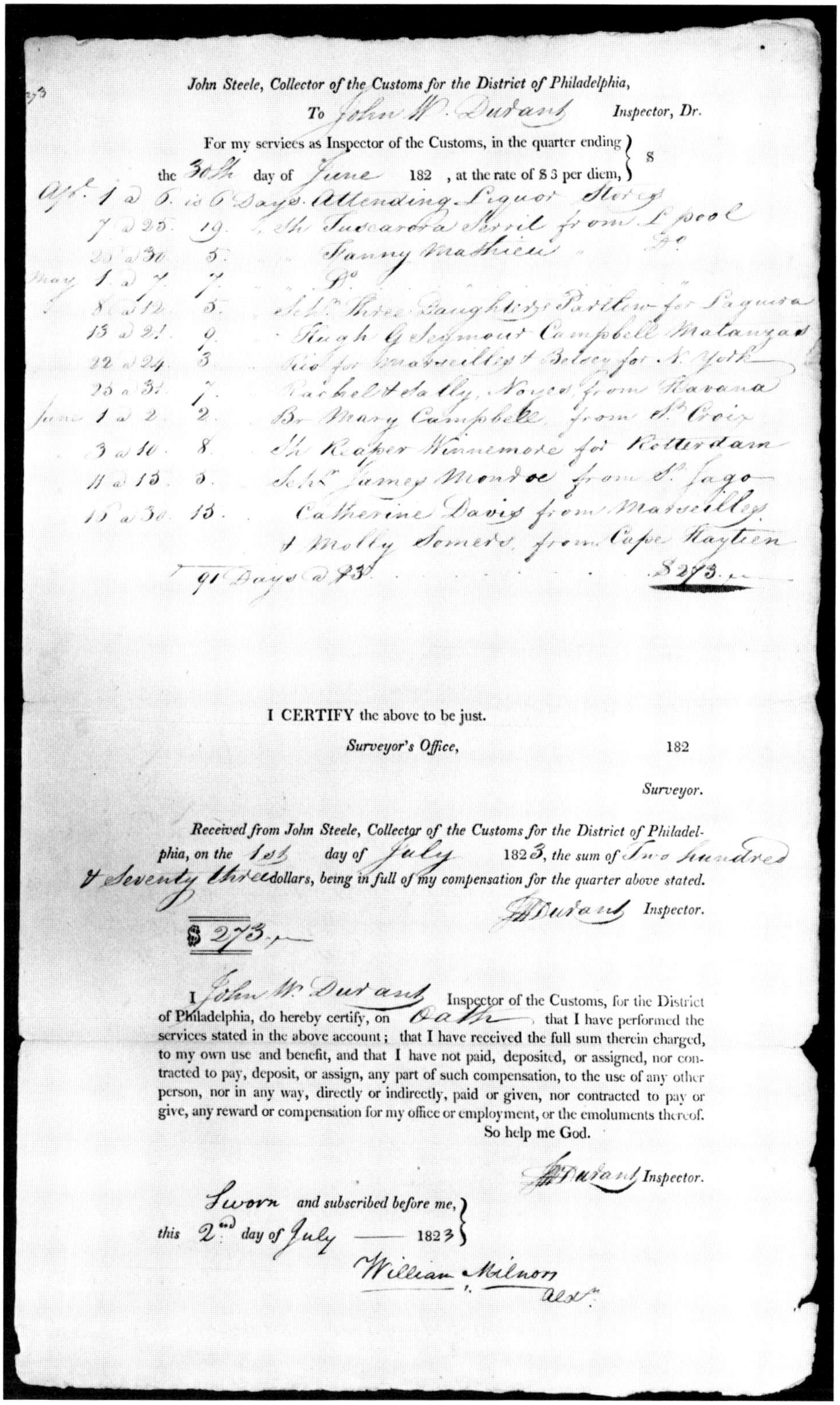

John Steele, Collector of the Customs for the District of Philadelphia,

To *John W. Durant* Inspector, Dr.

For my services as Inspector of the Customs, in the quarter ending the 30th day of *June* 182 , at the rate of $3 per diem,

[handwritten itemized list of days and services, partially legible:]

Apl. 1 a 6 — 6 Days Attending Liquor Store
7 a 25 — 19 — Sh Tuscarora Scovil from L'pool
25 a 30 — 5 — Fanny Mathieu Do
May 1 a 7 — 7 — Do
8 a 12 — 5 — Schr Three Daughters Barttow for Laguira
13 a 21 — 9 — Hugh & Seymour Campbell Matanzas
22 a 24 — 3 — Rio for Marseilles & Belsey for N. York
25 a 31 — 7 — Rachel & Sally Noyes from Havana
June 1 a 2 — 2 — Br Mary Campbell from St Croix
3 a 10 — 8 — Sh Roger Winnemore for Rotterdam
11 a 13 — 3 — Schr James Monroe from St Jago
15 a 30 — 15 — Catherine Davis from Marseilles
& Molly Somers from Cape Haytien

91 Days @ $3 — $273 .–

I CERTIFY the above to be just.

Surveyor's Office, 182

Surveyor.

Received from John Steele, Collector of the Customs for the District of Philadelphia, on the 1st day of *July* 1823, the sum of *Two hundred & Seventy three* dollars, being in full of my compensation for the quarter above stated.

Durant Inspector.

$273.–

I *John W. Durant* Inspector of the Customs, for the District of Philadelphia, do hereby certify, on *Oath* that I have performed the services stated in the above account; that I have received the full sum therein charged, to my own use and benefit, and that I have not paid, deposited, or assigned, nor contracted to pay, deposit, or assign, any part of such compensation, to the use of any other person, nor in any way, directly or indirectly, paid or given, nor contracted to pay or give, any reward or compensation for my office or employment, or the emoluments thereof. So help me God.

Durant Inspector.

Sworn and subscribed before me, this 2nd day of *July* — 1823

William Milnor
Alr

Inspector's Statement & Receipt: *Customs document providing a quarterly statement of services and a receipt for wages, relative to John Durant, an Inspector of the Customs in Philadelphia, 1823. Although not often found in maritime collections, such documents can provide valuable information about the duties and wages of customs employees, as well as insight into the organizational structure of the customs operation at a particular port.*

[CIRCULAR TO COLLECTORS AND NAVAL OFFICERS.]

TREASURY DEPARTMENT,

COMPTROLLERS' OFFICE,

January 22d, 1816.

SIR,

I HAVE been informed, from a very respectable source, that the House of Jackson, Alderson and Co. of Warrington, England, under fictitious Invoices, have attempted to force large quantities of Glass, from their Factory into the American market; instances of which have happened in the Port of Boston, and seizures thereof been made—It is stated that they have two Invoices, one to enter by, and one to sell by; the former from 30 to 50 per cent. less than the latter.—You will be vigilant in watching, particularly importations from this House, and put the Law rigorously in execution to detect ~~such~~ such Fraud, wherever you find just cause to suspect it.

With due respect,

Jos. Anderson

Treasury Department Circulars: *These Circulars (i.e., printed letters or announcements), were issued by the Treasury Department and sent out to the collectors at ports throughout the nation. It was the primary method used to keep each district abreast of the latest legislation and conditions affecting customs administration. Circulars often contain the signature of the Secretary of the Treasury.*

To qualify for drawback money, numerous documents were required. All were print-ed forms of various sizes, usually having little or no ornamentation. Several typefaces may be found on a single certificate, and many contain printing on both the front and the back. These forms remained fairly standardized between 1790-1860, with minor variations in size and style. Most of these documents were obtained through the customhouse, and carried the signatures of the collector and naval officer at the issuing port. Others would come from U.S. Consuls at foreign ports.

During its formative years, America did not have many finished products to export. Most domestic products and raw materials did not garner high profits for their exporters. One way in which Americans could make large profits, however, was to participate in the carrying trade, in which the more expensive products from the British and French West Indies (such as sugar) were bought by Americans and resold to Europeans. The first tariff law of 1789 recognized the importance of this carrying trade by providing for a refund, or Drawback, of virtually all duties paid on goods that were imported only to be exported within the year. Drawbacks made the carrying trade profitable.

Initial use of Drawback was not great, but when war broke out between England and France in 1793, Europe's need of the American carriers increased. To retain their neutral status, Americans had to declare West Indian goods in the United States before re-export-ing them to Europe as American goods. By 1798, the New York Customhouse was refund-ing as Drawbacks more than one-third of all duties collected.

To claim drawback monies, the importer first needed to obtain an entry of merchan-dise and one that certified his intention of exporting the cargo listed on the form of entry. If the goods were transferred within the United States, the new owner would also need to attest that he intended to export the cargo. If the cargo was transported along the coast, the owner had to obtain forms permitting him to do so. Lists of the transported cargo would be made at the original port and would be checked at the next port, provid-ing that the owner had obtained a form permitting him to unload the goods at those ports. The maximum number of coastwise transfers an owner could make was two, after which the Drawback could not be claimed. When the goods were exported, their owner could apply for a debenture in the amount of the Drawback, but he was required to sign a bond for twice that amount. The bond was released if proof of exportation, usually in the form of sworn statements by the consignee, the principal officers of the delivery vessel, and the American consul at the foreign port, arrived within the time specified within the bond, usually one or two years. Notary documents, swearing compliance with drawback regulations, might also be required to support an exporter's request for a rebate.

No Drawback could be obtained on some goods (a changing list) or on packages bro-ken or goods damaged while in the United States. Drawbacks did apply to imported goods that were used in American products that were exported, such as the molasses-rum conversion.

DRAWBACK FORMS AND CERTIFICATES

Entry of Merchandise Certificate: *This form indicates an Entry of Merchandise for coastwise transport. It states that the importers are in possession of goods that arrived in Philadelphia from Hamburg, Germany, and that they intend to ship that cargo to Baltimore for exportation. This one-page printed document details the cargo's movements as affirmed by the Collector, and was required in order to retain the right to drawback.*

(Certificate on the Exportation of Goods from a District other than the District of original Importation.)

No. _____

DISTRICT OF NEW-YORK—PORT OF NEW-YORK. *May 7* *Conn't,* 18*42*

We hereby Certify, That the Merchandise hereinafter specified, which were imported into the District of *Middletown Conn't,*
on the *twenty sixth* day of *July 1841* by *Joseph W Alsop Jr* in the *Bark Vondu* of
Ward Master, from *St Croix* and landed in this District in the month of *May 1842* out of the *Sloop Bella*
Brooks Master, from *Middletown* (having been previously entered at this office by
Alsop & Chauncy ,) have been exported hence by *them* in the *Brig Isabella* belonging to
Rd Hue Master, bound for *St Croix* having been previously inspected and *Guaged*
and that the said *Alsop & Chauncy* with *Richard Alsop* both of New-York, have entered into bond, in
pursuance of the law in that case made and provided.

MARKS.	NUMBERS.	PACKAGES, CONTENTS, AND RATES OF DUTIES.	AMOUNT OF DUTIES.
⊘	499 @ 502 532. 533 536. 541 546. 548 550. 552 614. 615 618 @ 622 634	Twenty Puncheons Rum Galls Dollars 644 - 2014 @ 53 1067.42 40 - 424.97 640.45 8 - 51.52	691.97

Amount of drawbacks payable, *Six hundred Ninety one Dollars Ninety seven Cents*

M Elliott NAVAL OFFICER.   *W Talman* COLLECTOR.

Certificate for Exporting Goods From a District Other Than the One of Original Importation: *This form notes the district of importation, the district of exportation, the final destination, and the master(s) and vessel(s) employed in transporting the cargo. The cargo was listed below the initial statement, with the amount of drawback appearing near the bottom of the certificate. Issued through the customhouse, the form carried the signatures of the collector and the naval officer.*

Bond on Exportation of Goods Eligible for Drawback: *This document indicates that Jacob Barker, Peleg Barker, and William H. Folger bound themselves for $35,870.00 to the United States in order to obtain drawback money for the goods exported and described in the Bond. The obligation was voided if or when proof of the cargo's arrival in Fayal was produced within one year. This was a one-page document, printed on both sides, containing the signatures of the bonded parties, the name of the vessel transporting the cargo, the destination, and the conditions for the proper execution of the Bond which were explained on the backside of the form. The Bond is essentially a statement by the receiver of the drawback that they will stand in bond for twice the amount of the debenture if the conditions specified within were not met.*

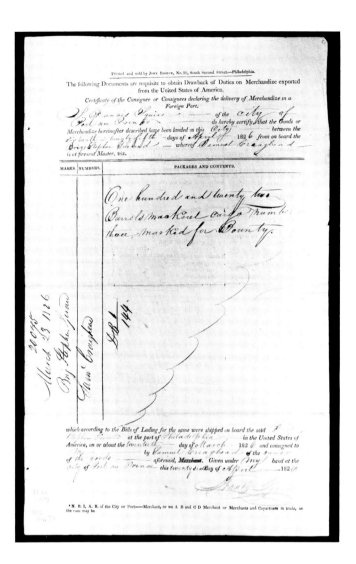

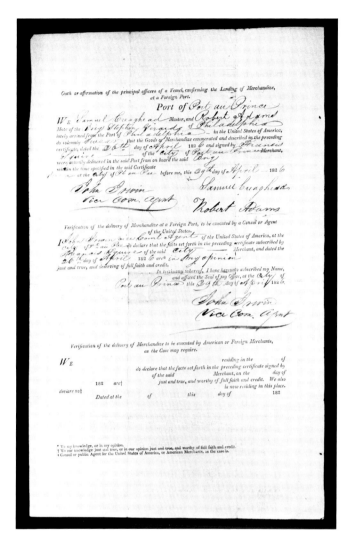

Debenture Certificate: *This is a one-page document, printed on both sides, containing four major parts: the Certificate of the Consignee, Oath of the master and mate, Consul's Certificate, and the Merchant's Certificate. The words "Debenture Certificate" generally do not appear on the document. When properly executed and returned to the exporter, the Debenture Certificate is final proof that those who exported the goods have complied with current drawback conditions, and can now be released from all required bonds or obligations to the United States. The illustrations show both sides of the document, which was probably executed as follows: On 23 March 1826 the master of the brig* Stephen Girard *signed in the margin, indicating that the cargo described therein was aboard. On 26 April 1826 the consignee signed the Certificate, stating that he had received the cargo at Port-au-Prince, which was unloaded between the sixteenth and twenty-fifth of April. Three days later the master and mate of the* Stephen Girard *sign the Oath affirming the consignee's statement. That same day the Vice Consul of the U.S. added his signature to verify the delivery of the cargo and confirm the accuracy of the Debenture Certificate. (Had there been no Consul assigned to the port of discharge an authorized merchant would have signed the vertification instead).*

ENROLMENT

Printed document of various sizes. Enrolment (spelled with one "l" on the document), contained some variation of the phrase, "...in conformity to an act of the Congress of the United States of America entitled, An Act for Enrolling and Licensing Ships or Vessels...." The word "Enrolment" is often printed prominently, and engraved eagles and other embellishments are frequently found on the earlier documents. The signatures of various customs officials are present, along with official stamps or seals.

By the Act of 18 February 1793, all vessels over 20 tons engaged in the domestic coasting trade or the fisheries, in order to be entitled to the privileges of ships of the United States, had to be enrolled. The document was issued by the customs surveyor, or the collector, and the enrollment qualifications and procedures were the same as those for registering ships. "And the same duties and authorities are given and imposed on all officers respectively in relation to such Enrollments,...and the ships so enrolled, with the master or owner, are subject to the same requisites, as are in those respects provided for ships registered." In addition, enrolled vessels carried a license for either fishing or coastal trade. A cash bond, the amount of which depended upon the size of the vessel, was necessary to enroll a vessel, and they could be revoked if the conditions of the document were violated. Enrolment Certificates are fairly common maritime manuscripts, and they can provide valuable information about a vessel or her owners.

ENROLMENT.

PERMANENT.

No. 1

Enrolment, in conformity to an Act of Congress of the UNITED STATES OF AMERICA, entitled, " *An Act for Enrolling and Licensing Ships or Vessels to be employed in the Coasting Trade and Fisheries, and for regulating the same;* " and of " *An Act to provide for the better security of the lives of passengers on board of vessels propelled, in whole or in part by steam,* " passed 7th JULY, 1838, and amended 30th AUGUST, 1852,

Paul Spofford off the City, County and State of New-York, having taken or subscribed the oath required by the said Act, and having sworn that

He the said Paul Spofford & Thomas Tileston of said place all

COLLECTOR.

Citizen of the United States, and sole owner of the Steam *Boat* or Vessel called the *Nashville* of *New York* whereof *Michael Berry* is at present master, and as he hath sworn, is a citizen of the United States, and the said Steam *Boat* or Vessel, was built at *New York* State of *New York* in the year one thousand eight hundred and *fifty three* as per *Certificate of William Collyer under whose direction she was built*

And *D. S. Benedict Ship Surveyor* having certified that the said Ship or Vessel has *No* decks and *No* mast and that her length is *Two hundred fifteen feet six inches* her breadth *thirty four feet six inches* her depth *Twenty one feet nine inches* and that she measures *Twelve Hundred & twenty 95/95* tons; *round* that she is a square-sterned *Steam Ship* has *a round tuck* no galleries and *a Billet* head; And that the said *Paul Spofford* having agreed to the description and admeasurement above specified, and sufficient security having been given according to the said Act, the said *Steam Ship* has been duly enrolled at the Port of New-York.

NAVAL OFFICER.

Given under our Hands and Seals, at the Port of New-York, this *4th* day of *January* in the year one thousand eight hundred and fifty *four*

An Enrolment Certificate for the steamboat Nashville, *4 January 1853. This was the first permanent Enrolment issued at the port of New York that year.*

DISTRICT OF NEWPORT.

Port of Newport, *december 27th 1797.*

I HEREBY certify that *John Turner* master of the *Sloop Fair American* of burthen *twenty three tons 48/95th parts of a Ton* owned by *the said John Turner* has surrendered to me a certificate of *Enrolment* granted to the said *Sloop* by *Wm. W. Morris dy.* collector of the customs for the district of *New York* numbered *267* dated *November 18th 1797* and a license to the said *Sloop* for carrying on the *coasting trade* granted by *the said Dy Collector* numbered *four hundred, seventy five* and dated *Novem: eighteenth, seventeen hundred & ninety seven.*

As witness my hand the day and year abovementioned.

Wm Ellery d/y Collr.

Certificate acknowledging the surrender of a sloop's Enrolment and License, signed by the Collector, December 27, 1797.

Per " ARABIA " Steamer.　　　　　　　　　　　Liverpool, 3rd April, 1857.

RATES OF FREIGHT FROM LIVERPOOL.

	Boston.		New York.		Philadelphia.		Baltimore.		Charleston.		New Orleans	
	s. d.	s. d.	s. d.	s. d.	s. d.	s. d.	s. d.	s. d.	s. d.	s. d.	s. d.	s. d.
Pig Iron, Bars, and Rails....	15 1	@17 6	11 0	@12 6	15 0	@17 6	15 0	@	15 0	@0 0	15 0	— 0 0
Salt...................	15 0	— 0 0	13 6	— 0 0	12 6	— 0 0	13 0	—14 0	7 0	nominal	11/ full Cargo.	12/6 limited q'ty
Dry Goods	15 0	—20 0	10 0	—17 6	15 0	—20 0	15 0	—20 0	20 0	@25 0	15 0	— 0 0
Hardware	20 0	— 0 0	12 6	— 0 0	20 0	—	20 0	— 0 0	0 0	—25 0	15 0	— 0 0
Earthenware		— 8 0	6 6	@0 0	9 0	— 0 0	9 0	— 0 0	6 0	— 0 0	0 0	— 0 0
Passengers	£4 10s. 0d. Gross.		£ 0s. @ £4 Gross.		£4 0s. Gross.		£4 @ £5. Nominal.		£5 0s. Gross.		£4 10s. Gross.	

COAL—FROM LIVERPOOL OR BIRKENHEAD.

To Bermuda ....15s. 0d.		To Constantinople ....25s. 0d.
„ Malta ....23s. 6d.		„ Trebisonde ....28s. 6d.
„ Trieste ....26s. 0d.		„ Sinope .. ..27s. 6d.
„ Corfu ....24s. 0d.		„ Ancona ....25s. 0d.
„ Smyrna ....25s. 0d.		„ Ragusa ....28s. 0d.
„ Varna ....27s. 6d.		„ Venice ....28s. 0d.
„ Gibraltar ....18s. 0d.		„ Messina ....21s. 0d.
„ Leghorn ....24s. 0d.		„ Genoa...............................23s. 6d.
„ Athens ....27s. 0d.		„ Naplos ....27s. 6d.
		„ Rhodes ....27s. 6d.

RAILS—BRISTOL CHANNEL.

To New Orleans................25s. @ 27/6 & 5°/₀		To City Point.......................30s. @ 31s. & 5°/₀
New York ....22/6 @ 25/0 „		Charleston.........................25/

GENERAL FREIGHTS.

Liverpool to Aden .. .. 32/6 Coal.	Home from Chincas, 80/ to U. K. for British vessels any size, or to London and Continent for Americans
„ Hong Kong .. .. 45/0 „	„ Calcutta 50s. to London or Liverpool, £5 all round.
Ceylon .. .. 30s. 0d. „	„ Bombay to Liverpool or London 55s. 0d.
„ Bombay .. .. 27s. 6d. „	„ Manilla ... .. 72/6 to U. K.
„ Suez .. .. 52/6 „	„ Moulmain 112s. 6d. to U. K., Teak.
„ Singapore .. .. 30s. 0d. „	King George's Sound from Wales 25s. 0d.
„ Shanghai .. .. 55s. 0d. „	Manilla .. .. „ „ 25s.
„ Calcutta, Rails, 27/6, Salt, 29s. 0d., Coal, 30s.	Sydney .. .. „ „ 37s. 6d.
„ Ascension .. .. .. 21s. „	
„ Fernando Po .. .. .. 23s. 6d. „	
„ Callao .. .. 20s. 0d. nominal „	
„ Sydney .. .. 37s. 6d. Coal. „	
„ Coquimbo .. .. 21s. 6d. „	
Melbourne from Wales 40s. assorted cargo, Coals, Iron and Coke.	

JACOT, TAYLOR & TIPPER,
SHIP BROKERS.

Freight Circulars were printed at large ports by agents or brokers, most often on a weekly basis. They provided the latest information on current prices, and the availability of enumerated goods at that port. These Circulars were mailed out to shippers or potential clients, in order to keep them updated on market conditions. They were also known in some places as "price-current" sheets or "market reviews."

FREIGHT LIST

Printed document of various sizes and formats. Like the manifest, the Freight List has printed columns for the names of shippers and consignees, packages, and their marks and contents. Unlike the manifest, however, a Freight List records the rate at which the transported cargo will be charged, the cost levied for freight and primage, and the final sum due from either the shipper or the consignee. It is a private business document and was not certified or signed by any public official. "Freight List" usually appears in bold print, and the name of the agent executing the document is often present.

The terms "freight" and "cargo" are often misunderstood. Freight is the sum paid by a shipper who hires a vessel to transport his goods, and cargo is the term for the goods transported. Manifests and invoices are primarily concerned with cargo, while Freight Lists provide a record of the charges assessed for the shipment of cargo. Three kinds of charges were assessed: general charges, freight, and primage. General charges were assessed for any unusual expenses that had been incurred in transporting the cargo. Freight was a charge generally levied on the principle that the merchant was paying for the use of the ship (or part of a ship) for a specific time. Although it was usually assessed by the weight or volume of his cargo, it was possible for shippers to owe freight money simply because they had reserved the use of part of the vessel, regardless of whether they had actually filled it. Primage, the third charge, was for the care of the goods during transport, typically assessed at 5 to 15 percent of the freight. Originally it was a gratuity for the captain, but by the mid-nineteenth century it was paid to the owners. These three charges were collected together, from either the shipper or consignee. The responsible party was designated in the Charter Party or the Bill of Lading. Consequently the Freight List was essentially a business document between the shipper, the consignee, and the vessel transporting the cargo.

JONES, MACKINDER & CO., COMMISSION MERCHANTS AND SHIP BROKERS,
91 Gravier Street, New Orleans.

FREIGHT LIST of Ship *General Berry* Capt. *Nathan Seavey* from New Orleans, to *Glasgow*

No.	SHIPPERS	CONSIGNEES	MARKS	PACKAGES AND CONTENTS	BUSHELS	WEIGHT	RATE	CHARGES	FREIGHT	PRIMAGE	TOTAL
1	Stewart & Co	order	Various	509 Five Hundred & Nine Bales Cotton		255,746	4d		466 2 9	23 6 2	489 8 11
2	"	"	D U	100 One Hundred Bales Cotton		41,975	"		87 9 0	4 7 5	91 16 5
3	"	"	B V Q M ⊞	259 Two Hundred & Fifty Nine Bales Cotton		105,242	"		225 14 3	11 5 8	236 19 11
4	Clason & Co	"	W	30 Thirty Bales Cotton		12,542	"		26 1 4	1 6 1	27 7 5
5	Joseph Johnston	"	2 U S 8 U R	90 Ninety Bales Cotton		40,008	"		83 7 0	4 3 4	87 10 4
6	Stewart & Co	"	X D	109 One Hundred & Nine Bales Cotton		47,330	7/6		86 5 7	4 6 3	90 11 10
7	Juan & M. Egana	"	B	998 Nine Hundred & Ninety Eight bbls. Flour			3/6		174 13 0	8 14 7	183 7 7
8	A & J. L. Mills	"	A	790 Seven Hundred & Ninety bbls. Flour			2/		79 0 0	3 19 0	82 19 0
9	Abr. McVicar	"	15 00 C V	Ten bbls. Flour & Two bbls. Hams					1 4 0	1 2	1 5 2
10	R. S. Mann & Co	Thomas Callender		849 Eight Hundred & Forty Nine bdls. Md. Hides			1/6		63 13 6	3 2 7	66 17 1
								£	1293 10 5	64 13 3	1358 3 8

New Orleans. 12. May. 1857
Jones, Mackinder & Co.
Per Thomas B. Hood.

This Freight List for an 1857 voyage from New Orleans to Glasgow lists the shippers and consignees and the charges assessed for the transportation of their goods. Printed on the form is the name of the agent whose business it was to bring cargoes and available vessels together.

LETTER OF MARQUE/PRIVATEER COMMISSION

Usually a printed document, issued in various dimensions, containing the signature of the President of Congress (during the American Revolution), and later signed by the President of the United States and Secretary of State. There is a general absence of decorative engraving, but these forms will display the United States seal and the usual customs stamps, signatures, etc.

Letters of Marque were licenses granted by a monarch or government to privately-owned vessels, enabling them under certain conditions to war against the shipping of an enemy nation. The word marque, from the French, was used in this sense to mean a pledge to seize or capture. Vessels carrying these documents were popularly known as privateers.

There were nearly 800 American privateers commissioned during the Revolutionary War, 365 during the period of the undeclared war with France, *ca.* 1798-1800, and more than 500 sailed against the British during the War of 1812. In the most limited terms, a privateer was a private armed vessel carrying no cargo, devoted exclusively to warlike use, and operating under a commission obtained from the government. Some of these commissions were called Letters of Marque, and were issued to armed cargo-carrying vessels authorizing them to engage enemy shipping during the course of their commercial voyages. By 1812, Letters of Marque and Privateer Commissions were essentially the same document, and it is certainly not grossly incorrect to refer to all such vessels as privateers.

Application and issuance procedures varied from one period to another. During the American Revolution the Continental Congress adopted a printed form with blank spaces for the name of the vessel, owners and master, and figures for tonnage, guns and crew. These blank commissions, signed by the President of Congress, were sent out to the United Colonies, who assumed primary responsibility for the regulation and conduct of their own privateer fleets. By 1812 a shipowner applied in writing to the Collector, or in some cases directly to the State Department. If approved, he would then sign a bond, usually for a sum ranging between $5,000 and $10,000 (depending upon the size of his vessel or crew) to insure his ship's compliance with the conditions of the Letter of Marque or Privateer Commission. The document itself, containing the signatures of the President and the Secretary of State, was then issued to the shipowner through the Customs Service, and remained valid until recalled by the government or canceled through a violation of the bond.

Letters of Marque were abolished by the Congress of Paris in 1856, and the practice of privateering was considered obsolete by the end of the nineteenth century. Letters of Marque and Privateer's Commissions can be considered truly unique and valuable items in any maritime collection.

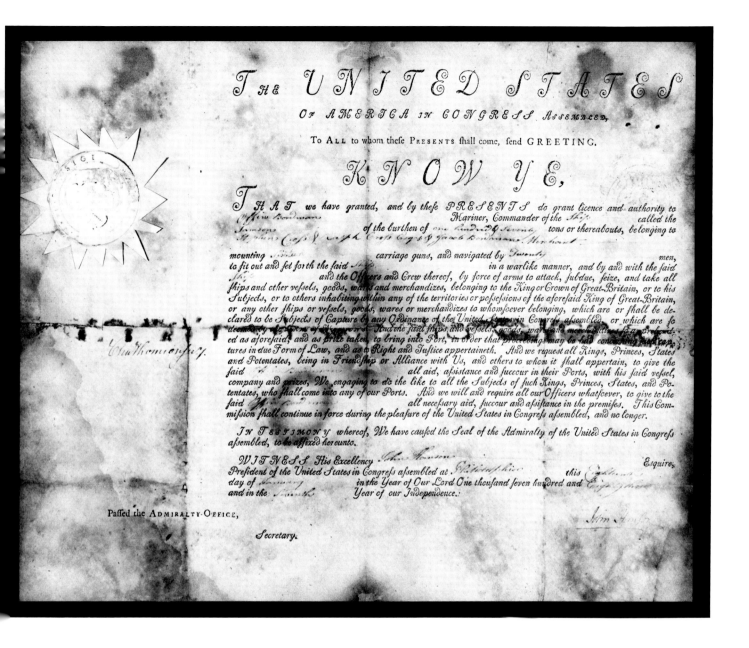

Commission granted by the "United States in Congress assembled" *to the ship* Samson *during the American Revolution. The words Letter of Marque and privateer do not appear on the document, but its identity is made clear by instructions for the vessel "to fit out and set forth...in a warlike manner...and by force of arms to attack, subdue, seize, and take all ships and other vessels...belonging to the King or Crown of Great Britain...." The document measures approximately 16" x 13", is printed on heavy grade paper, and displays the congressional seal in the upper left-hand corner. (Mss. Coll., Peabody Museum, Salem, MA. Photo by Mark Sexton.)*

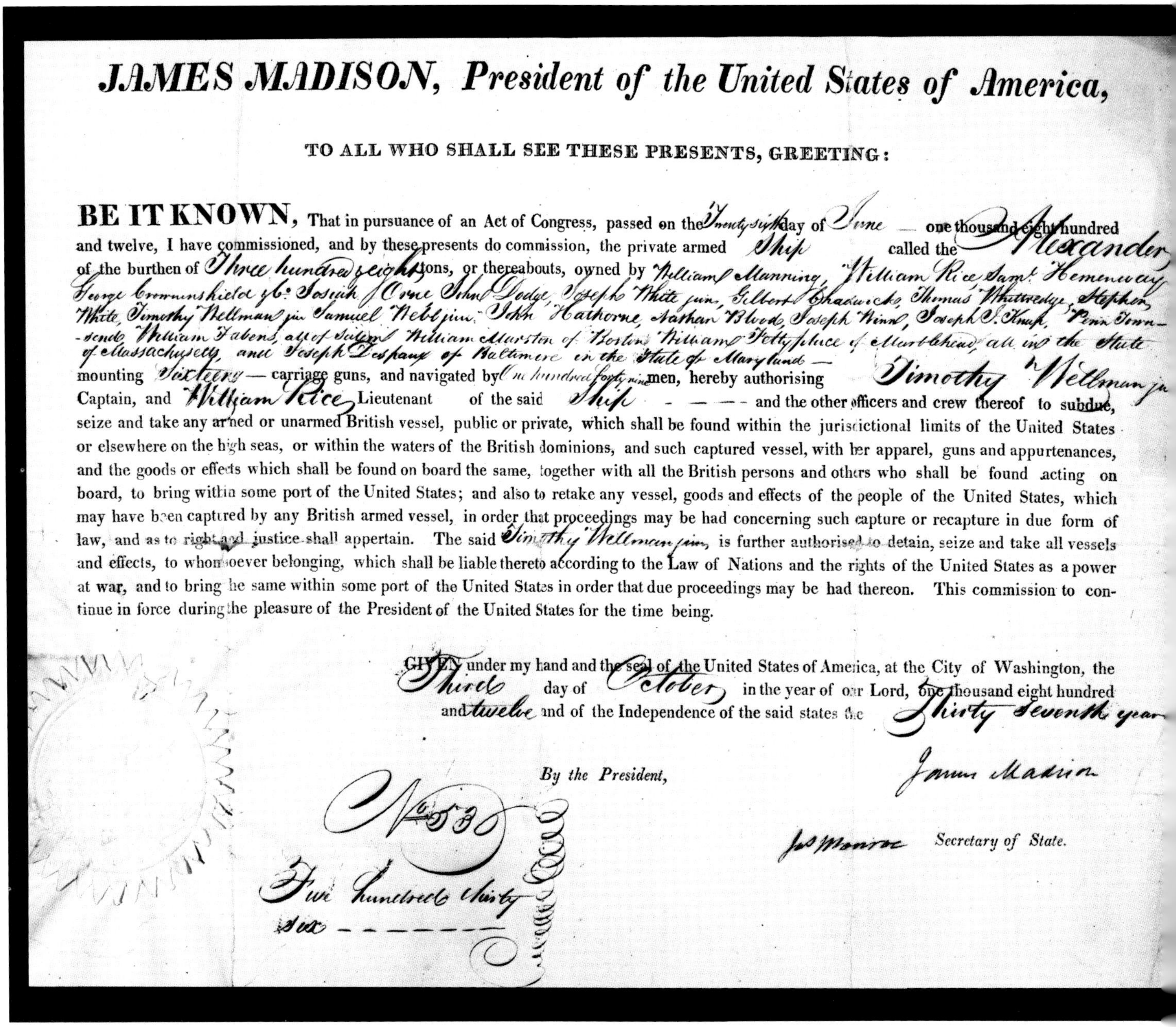

LETTER OF MARQUE/PRIVATEER COMMISSION

JAMES MADISON, President of the United States of America,

TO ALL WHO SHALL SEE THESE PRESENTS, GREETING:

BE IT KNOWN, That in pursuance of an Act of Congress, passed on the *Twenty-sixth* day of *June* — one thousand eight hundred and twelve, I have commissioned, and by these presents do commission, the private armed *Ship* called the *Alexander* of the burthen of *Three hundred eight* tons, or thereabouts, owned by *William Manning, William Rice, Sam.ᵗ Hemenway, George Crowninshield &c. Josiah P. Orne, John Dodge, Joseph White jun, Gilbert Chadwicke, Thomas Whittredge, Stephen White, Timothy Wellman jr. Samuel Webb jun. John Hathorne, Nathan Blood, Joseph Winn, Joseph J. Knap, Penn Townsend, William Fabens, all of Salem, William Marston of Boston, William Petty place of Marblehead, all in the State of Massachusetts, and Joseph Despaux of Baltimore in the State of Maryland —* mounting *Sixteen* — carriage guns, and navigated by *One hundred forty nine* men, hereby authorising *Timothy Wellman jr.* Captain, and *William Rice* Lieutenant of the said *Ship* — — — and the other officers and crew thereof to subdue, seize and take any armed or unarmed British vessel, public or private, which shall be found within the jurisdictional limits of the United States or elsewhere on the high seas, or within the waters of the British dominions, and such captured vessel, with her apparel, guns and appurtenances, and the goods or effects which shall be found on board the same, together with all the British persons and others who shall be found acting on board, to bring within some port of the United States; and also to retake any vessel, goods and effects of the people of the United States, which may have been captured by any British armed vessel, in order that proceedings may be had concerning such capture or recapture in due form of law, and as to right and justice shall appertain. The said *Timothy Wellman jun,* is further authorised to detain, seize and take all vessels and effects, to whomsoever belonging, which shall be liable thereto according to the Law of Nations and the rights of the United States as a power at war, and to bring the same within some port of the United States in order that due proceedings may be had thereon. This commission to continue in force during the pleasure of the President of the United States for the time being.

GIVEN under my hand and the seal of the United States of America, at the City of Washington, the *Third* day of *October,* in the year of our Lord, one thousand eight hundred and *twelve* and of the Independence of the said states the *Thirty Seventh* year.

By the President,

James Madison

Jas Monroe Secretary of State.

No 536

Five hundred thirty six

By 1812 the distinction between a Letter of Marque and a Privateer's Commission was difficult to establish. Often the vessel's description (i.e. number of guns or the size of her crew) is the most accurate indicator as to whether it was an armed merchantman or a private warship. The document illustrated here, belonging to the ship Alexander, is typical of the commissions granted by the government during the War of 1812. Printed on heavy grade paper, approximately 16" x 13". (Mss. Coll., Peabody Museum, Salem, MA. Photo by Mark Sexton.)

No 57 –

Know all Men by these presents,

THAT WE _Henry Smith, Samuel James & Samuel Pallin all merchants of the town & County of Providence in the State of Rhode Island &c –_

Owner **s** of the private armed vessel of _Providence called the "Providence" navigated with fifty_ men and _Nicholas Hopkins mariner of said Providence_ Commander of the same _and Samuel Metcalf of the same Providence merchant and Christopher Ellery Esquire of Cranston as Sureties both in the aforesaid County of Providence_

are held and firmly bound to the United States of America, in the penal sum of _five_ ————————————————— thousand dollars, money of the United States, to the payment whereof we bind ourselves jointly and severally, our joint and several heirs, executors and administrators. Witness our hands and seals this _eighth_ day of _August_ in the year of our Lord 18/_2_ .

The condition of the above obligation is such, that whereas the President of the United States hath this day commissioned the said private armed vessel as a letter of marque and reprisal; now if the owner, officers and crew of the said armed vessel shall observe the treaties and laws of the United States, and the instructions which shall be given them according to law for the regulation of their conduct, and satisfy all damages and injuries which shall be done or committed contrary to the tenor thereof by such vessel during her commission, and deliver up the same when revoked by the President of the United States, then this obligation shall be void, and otherwise remain in full force.

Signed, sealed and delivered in presence of us.

Wm Peckham Jr

Henry Smith

Saml James

Saml P Allin

Nicholas Hopkins

Chris A Ellery

Saml. Metcalf

Bond for a Letter of Marque _signed by the master and owners of the "private armed vessel"_ Providence, _8 August 1812. Bonds were intended to insure compliance with the instructions and regulations specified in the commission or Letter of Marque. In this example, the signatories are bonded to the United States for the sum of five thousand dollars until such time as the document is recalled by the President. (Courtesy of Rhode Island Historical Society.)_

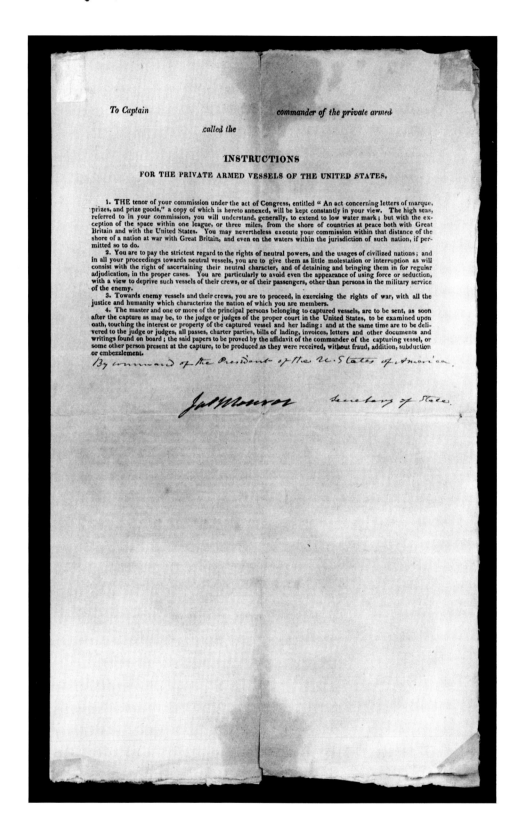

To Captain   commander of the private armed

called the

INSTRUCTIONS

FOR THE PRIVATE ARMED VESSELS OF THE UNITED STATES,

1. THE tenor of your commission under the act of Congress, entitled " An act concerning letters of marque, prizes, and prize goods," a copy of which is hereto annexed, will be kept constantly in your view. The high seas, referred to in your commission, you will understand, generally, to extend to low water mark; but with the exception of the space within one league, or three miles, from the shore of countries at peace both with Great Britain and with the United States. You may nevertheless execute your commission within that distance of the shore of a nation at war with Great Britain, and even on the waters within the jurisdiction of such nation, if permitted so to do.

2. You are to pay the strictest regard to the rights of neutral powers, and the usages of civilized nations; and in all your proceedings towards neutral vessels, you are to give them as little molestation or interruption as will consist with the right of ascertaining their neutral character, and of detaining and bringing them in for regular adjudication, in the proper cases. You are particularly to avoid even the appearance of using force or seduction, with a view to deprive such vessels of their crews, or of their passengers, other than persons in the military service of the enemy.

3. Towards enemy vessels and their crews, you are to proceed, in exercising the rights of war, with all the justice and humanity which characterize the nation of which you are members.

4. The master and one or more of the principal persons belonging to captured vessels, are to be sent, as soon after the capture as may be, to the judge or judges of the proper court in the United States, to be examined upon oath, touching the interest or property of the captured vessel and her lading: and at the same time are to be delivered to the judge or judges, all passes, charter parties, bills of lading, invoices, letters and other documents and writings found on board; the said papers to be proved by the affidavit of the commander of the capturing vessel, or some other person present at the capture, to be produced as they were received, without fraud, addition, subduction or embezzlement.

By command of the President of the U. States of America.

Ja% Monroe   *Secretary of State.*

Instructions to accompany Letters of Marque *were given to the commanders of these private armed vessels after the bond was signed and the commission was obtained. The example illustrated here was attached to a copy of the Act Concerning Letters of Marque, Prizes and Prize Goods, passed in June, 1812, which further outlined the conduct of American privateers on the high seas. It displays the signature of James Monroe, Secretary of State.*

Printed document of various sizes and formats. "License" was often prominently printed near the top of the document. Signatures of customs officials are present, and there is a general absence of decorative engraving.

This License was a product of the Act of 1793 entitled, "An Act for enrolling and licensing Ships or Vessels to be employed in the Coasting Trade and Fisheries, and for regulating the same." It was issued through the Customs Service to vessels, regardless of size, authorizing them to engage in either fishing or the coastal trade for a period of one year. Any vessel licensed for these trades that exceeded 20 tons would also need to have an Enrollment Certificate. Registered vessels were not required to have a license. These documents are frequently found in maritime collections.

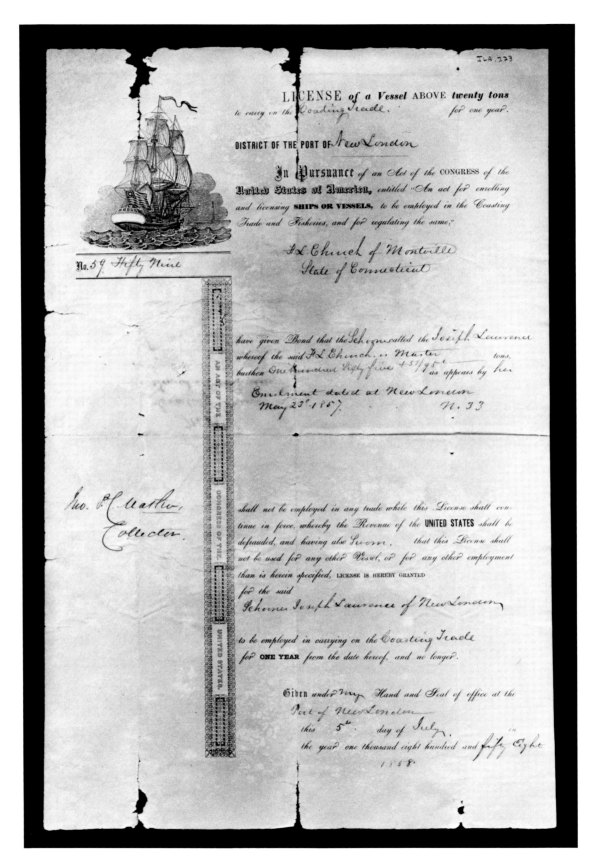

License for a vessel above 20 tons, *to carry on the coasting trade for a period of one year, signed by the Collector at New London, Connecticut, 5 July 1858. It was the 59th License issued at that port during the year.*

I _Winthrop Stanwood_ DO SOLEMNLY SWEAR, that I am a citizen of the United States ; and I furthermore ſwear, that the Licence now granted to the _Boat Lucy_ of _Gloucester_ and of which veſſel I am the Maſter, ſhall not be uſed for any other veſſel, or any other employment, than that for which it is ſpecially granted ; or in any other trade or buſineſs, whereby the revenue of the United States may be defrauded. So help me God. _Winthrop Stanwood_

COLLECTOR'S OFFICE,
Diſtrict of _Gloucester December 9th 1795_

Sworn to and ſubſcribed.

Wm Tuck Collector.

Master's Oath upon granting a vessel's License, *signed by the Collector at Gloucester, Massachusetts, 9 December 1795. The shipmaster also signed the document, within which he affirms his American citizenship and swears not to use his vessel in a manner that would violate the conditions of the License.*

***License authorizing the ship* Warren** *to engage in the coasting trade, "or to carry on the Bank or Whale Fishery" for a period of one year. Dated 1790, it is an example of the kind of document issued by the Customs Service before the Federal Licensing Act was passed in 1793. Over the years Licenses became more specific, indicating a vessel's employment in the coasting trade, the cod fishery, mackerel fishery, etc. (Courtesy of Rhode Island Historical Society.)*

A ship's Logbook, as opposed to a journal or diary, was the official record of a voyage. While a journal could be kept by any crew member, the Logbook was most often kept by the mate, or first officer. It was the official record of the ship's voyage.

Logbooks recorded information that was of concern to the ship: speed, distance, course, wind, weather, and any events which may have had consequence on the voyage. Information was often collected on watch by the mate in charge, and the data recorded on the log slate or chalk board at the end of the "day" (a sea day being 12 noon to 12 noon). The first mate showed the information on the log slate to the master for any corrections or additions, after which he transcribed the data into the Logbook. The mate, in the process of transcription, was to note the master's changes, if any. Should damage occur to the ship or cargo during the voyage, the Logbook would contain an accurate description of the events leading to the loss. The information would be of great value to the owners and to insurers when determining liabilities and settlements. Logbooks could also provide substantial evidence for any legal proceedings brought against the owners, officers, or crew members. However, despite the legal implications, Logbooks were rarely kept as meticulously during the first half of the 19th century as was outlined in such contemporary guides as *The Shipmaster's Assistant.*

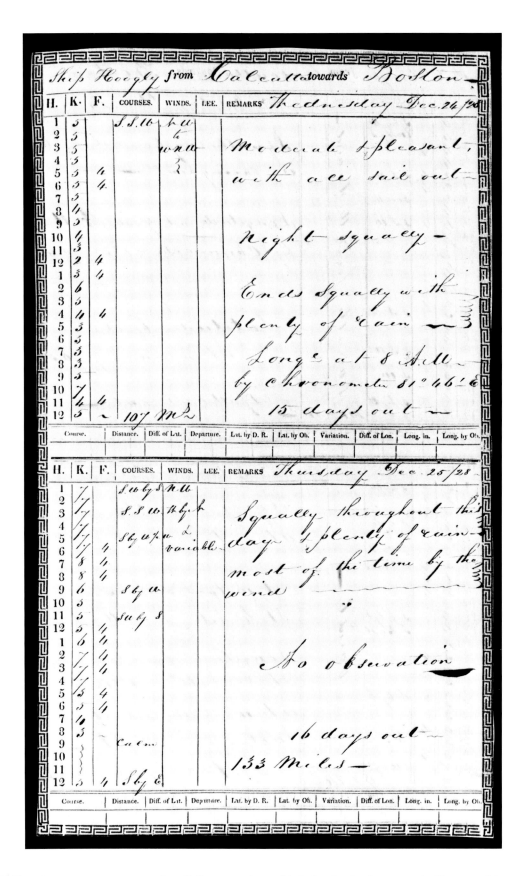

While there was no standard format *for a ship's Logbook, the example illustrated here was frequently used during the early 1800s. The titles of the various printed columns provide an accurate indication of the kinds of information recorded in these volumes.*

Printed document of various sizes and formats. A typical Manifest would have columns for marks and numbers, packages and contents, numbers of entries, shipper, consignee, etc., in addition to the vessel's name and home port, tonnage, owner's names, and the ports of departure and destination. Included also is a sworn statement of accuracy, signed by the master, and verified with a statement signed by the collector. These statements are often found on the backside of the smaller documents. Small engravings are also occasionally found.

A Manifest is the detailed statement or invoice of a vessel's cargo. It includes such information as the Bills of Lading numbers, the numbers of packages and their identifying marks, the names of the shippers and consignees, ports of destination, etc. More specifically there are outward (or clearing Manifests), inward Manifests, coasting Manifests, and passenger Manifests. The kind of information required could vary somewhat from one kind of Manifest to another, but their purpose was the same. This was the official document consulted when any legal action might be necessary relative to a vessel's cargo. The Manifest, properly made out and sworn to by the master, had to be presented to the collector, consul, or other appropriate authority, before a ship entered or cleared port. Manifests are fairly common maritime documents, and they can be an informative research source for the maritime historian.

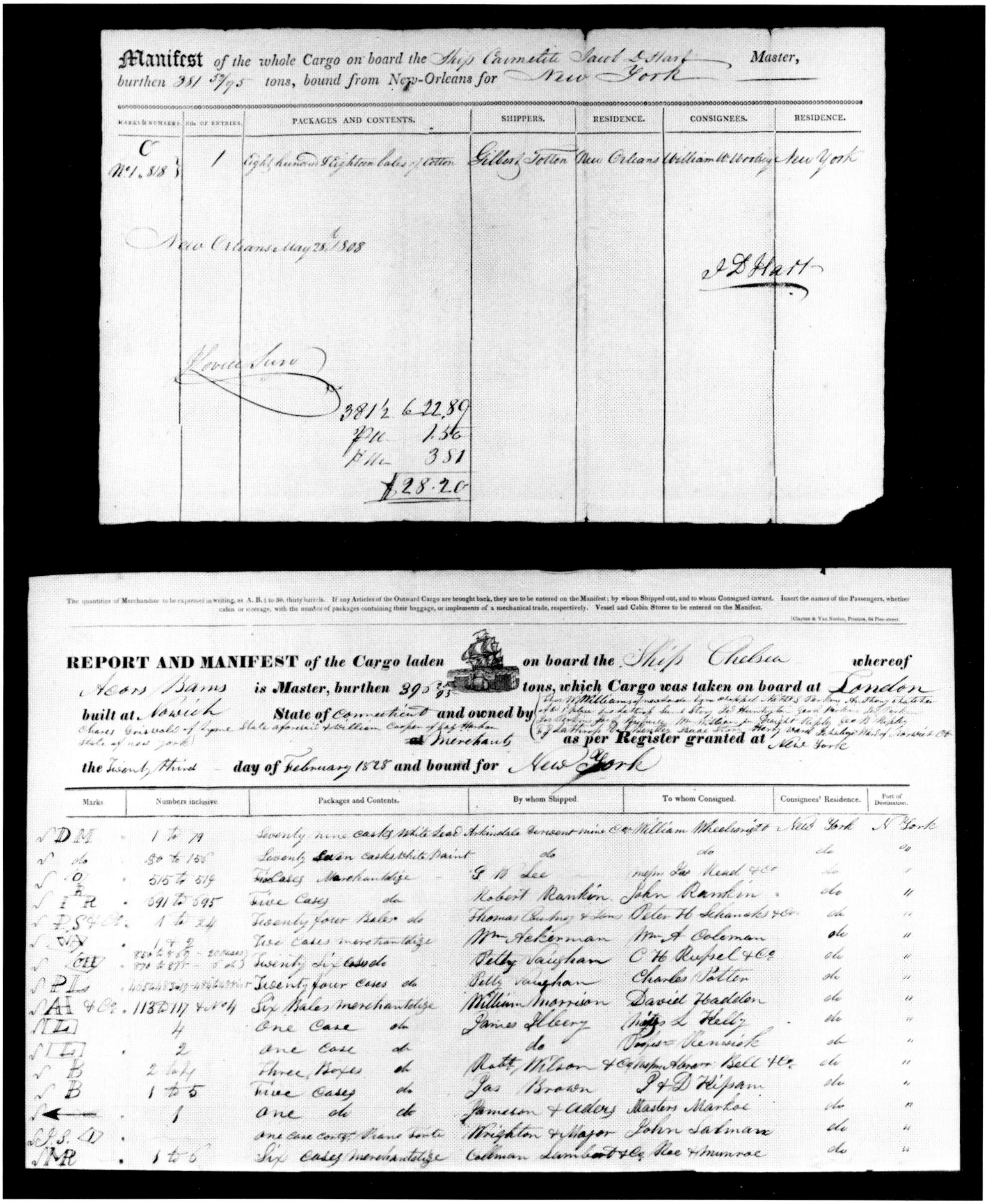

Manifest *of the whole Cargo on board the* Ship Carmelite Jacob D. Hart *Master, burthen* 381 57/95 *tons, bound from New-Orleans for* New York

MARKS & NUMBERS.	NO. OF ENTRIES.	PACKAGES AND CONTENTS.	SHIPPERS.	RESIDENCE.	CONSIGNEES.	RESIDENCE.
C Nº 1. 818	1	Eight hundred & Eighteen bales of cotton	Gilbert Totten	New Orleans	William W. Woolsey	New York

New Orleans May 28. 1808

J D Hart

381½ 6 22.89
156
381
$28.20

The quantities of Merchandise to be expressed in writing, as A. B. 1 to 50, thirty barrels. If any Articles of the Outward Cargo are brought back, they are to be entered on the Manifest; by whom Shipped out, and to whom Consigned inward. Insert the names of the Passengers, whether cabin or steerage, with the number of packages containing their baggage, or implements of a mechanical trade, respectively. Vessel and Cabin Stores to be entered on the Manifest.

Clayton & Van Norden, Printers, 64 Pine-street.

REPORT AND MANIFEST *of the Cargo laden on board the* Ship Chelsea *whereof* Acors Barns *is Master, burthen* 395 ⅔₅ *tons, which Cargo was taken on board at* London *built at* Norwich *State of* Connecticut *and owned by* [illegible] Merchants *as per Register granted at* New York *the* Twenty third *day of* February 1828 *and bound for* New York

Marks	Numbers inclusive	Packages and Contents.	By whom Shipped	To whom Consigned.	Consignees' Residence.	Port of Destination.
DM	1 to 79	Seventy nine casks White Lead	Arkindale Vencent mine Co	William Wheelwright	New York	N York
do	80 to 156	Seventy seven casks White Paint	do	do	do	do
O	515 to 519	Five Cases Merchandize	G W Lee	Messrs Jas Mead & Co	do	"
I R	591 to 595	Five Cases do	Robert Rankin	John Rankin	do	"
P S & Co	1 to 24	Twenty four Bales do	Thomas Courtney & Sons	Peter H Schenck & Co	do	"
WA	1 & 2	Two Cases merchandize	Wm Ackerman	Wm A Coleman	do	"
CH	850 to 869 – 20 cases; 870 to 875 – 6 do	Twenty six cases do	Pelly Vaughan	C H Russel & Co	do	"
PL	[illegible]	Twenty four cases do	Pelly Vaughan	Charles Potter	do	"
A & Co	113 to 117 & No 4	Six Bales merchandize	William Morrison	David Hadden	do	"
L	4	One Case do	James Illery	[illegible] L Kelly	do	"
L	2	One Case do	do	Poyer Renwick	do	"
B	2 to 4	Three Boxes do	Robt Wilson & Co	Messrs Abram Bell & Co	do	"
B	1 to 5	Five Cases do	Jas Brown	P & D Hispam	do	"
←	1	One do do	Jameson & Aders	Masters Markoe	do	"
I.S. D		One case contg Piano forte	Wrighton & Major	John Salman	do	"
MR	1 to 6	Six cases merchandize	Collman Lambert & Co	Rae & Munroe	do	"

Manifests like the ones illustrated here *are commonly found in collections of maritime business papers. The one from New Orleans in 1808 is for a cargo of 818 bales of cotton, New Orleans to New York. The other is a Manifest (only the upper half shown) for a large general cargo shipped from London to New York in 1828. The uniform handwriting on this document would indicate that it was probably the official copy taken aboard the vessel and produced upon arrival.*

Marine Insurance Policy

Most often a printed document of one or more pages, varying in size and composition. It indicated the standard terms and securities, with blanks provided for conditions unique to a particular policy. Other information would include the name of the vessel insured and the master, a description of the cargo (if insured), the stated value of the insured, the term of the policy, the policy number, the premium, etc.

Marine insurance in colonial America was underwritten primarily by wealthy citizens who pledged to pay a portion of the vessel's or cargo's value if it was lost. The owner of a vessel contracted to compensate the underwriters at a specified rate for this protection. This contract was the Marine Insurance Policy. The first United States incorporated company for marine insurance was chartered in 1794, and several others were in business by the end of the century. During the early 1800s these companies suffered from European abuses of our neutral shipping and their losses were frequently severe. However, the business of marine insurance continued to grow and was firmly established by the mid-nineteenth century.

Marine Insurance Policies are often found in maritime collections. As research sources, these documents can provide information about the current values of ships and cargoes, as well as how various forces affected the safety of American shipping.

Policy No. 2446 issued by the Warren Insurance Company, of Warren, Rhode Island, *for $1,400 on the schooner* Chance *at a rate of 9% for twelve months, 27 October 1828, is typical of the kind often found in maritime collections of this period.*

Documents Relative to Maritime Insurance Claims

Since the owners of the vessel and cargo did not usually escort their interests to their destination, the responsibility to initiate the claims process for loss or damage fell to the shipmaster. When these losses – termed "Averages" – occurred, the first action taken by the master upon arrival in port was to file a Note of Protest. This document was made before a notary public, consul, or other qualified official, by the master within twenty-four hours of the vessel's arrival. It is a short document, providing the briefest account of the circumstances that caused the damages, and could also include a description of the damage suffered. The primary reason for making a Note of Protest was to establish the right to extend the protest in the future should it become necessary.

This extension of the protest, commonly referred to as a "Protest" was usually a more lengthy and detailed document, describing all the circumstances surrounding the average; the date, the time, the setting and striking of all sails, a characterization of the weather responsible for the damage, what was damaged, what was sacrificed for the mutual good, etc. It was intended to be a clear and accurate statement of the events of the voyage, and was executed before a qualified public official by the master accompanied by one or two other crew members who could vouch for and support the master's account.

The Protest was important because it provided the insurer with the information required for them to properly evaluate a claim. In addition it also released "the vessel from liability for damage to cargo or other claims."

In addition to the Protest, the master arranged for a survey of the vessel and/or cargo. Prior to having the survey done he should have inspected his vessel and made his own list of damages. Supplying this list to the surveyors could often insure a more accurate survey. Underwriters often had agents appointed in many major ports throughout the world who would assist in the selection of surveyors.

The result of the survey was a Survey Certificate, made out by the surveyors for the vessel or the cargo, which included a description of the damage and probable cause of same. A statement regarding the current condition of the vessel might be found, along with recommendations that certain repairs be made. The recommendations, however, were only advice; the master was in no way obligated to follow them.

A popular method of acquiring funds for repair without the assistance of the owners was through the use of Bottomry and Respondentia Bonds. This was expensive and the amount borrowed was limited as much as possible. In these circumstances a shipmaster borrowed the money necessary for repair from some individual or company in the port where he was, bonding the vessel (Bottomry) and/or the cargo and freight (Respondentia) as collateral for the loan. Premiums on Bottomry and Respondentia Bonds were high, since the lender was taking a large risk. If the vessel was subsequently lost before she returned to her home port, the lender lost everything, because the owner was not obligated to repay his debt. These creditors, however, could often obtain insurance on the amount loaned under Bottomry.

In maritime terms the word "average" is used to identify damages and expenses resulting from "perils to navigation" encountered during a voyage. More specifically there is General Average and Particular Average.

The average (i.e. loss) suffered by the voluntary sacrifice of cargo is known as General Average. Thus if a consignee's cargo was jettisoned in order to save the ship and the rest of the cargo, it would seem only right that the other consignees compensate the one suffering the loss, since they benefited from the act. The idea of general average contribution was founded upon the principle of co-partnership between the owners of a ship and cargo, for mutual protection, and limited liability against the extraordinary dangers of sea travel. Expenditures accrued by the vessel as a result of the damages, such as towage, wharfage fees, surveyor's fees, and adjustment fees, were also included in the scope of general average. The amount contributed by each co-partner to the total in the event of a sacrifice was directly proportional to the value of his cargo after it was saved.

General Average was in no way connected with a policy of marine insurance. A contribution was required of every interested party regardless of whether or not they were insured. Particular Average, on the other hand, was an average, i.e. loss, accidental in character arising from one of the many perils encountered at sea, against which the assured was insured. Particular Average had everything to do with an insurance contract, and formed the basis of the insurance claim. The survey of the vessel, cargo, and freight, formed part of the general and particular averages, with additional expenditures accrued in consequence of the damages comprising the remainder.

Following a complete accounting of the damages to the voyage, a lengthy statement was prepared which detailed the loss, expenditures, and ultimate contribution of each individual concerned in the average adjustment. This statement, frequently found in maritime collections, has been called a General Average Statement; Statement of General and Particular Average; Statement of General Average and Partial Loss; and various combinations of same. It is a private business document, often encompassing insured losses and contributions under the principle of general average, which together satisfied all claims in a case of partial loss. This adjustment was often completed at the vessel's home port, where many of the principal parties were frequently found.

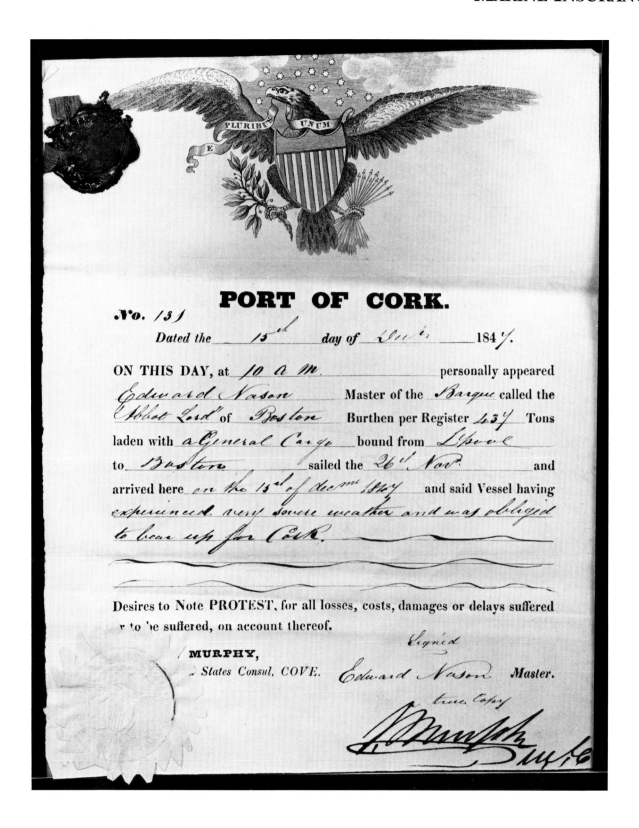

PORT OF CORK.

No. 131

Dated the _____ 15th _____ day of _____ Decr _____ 1847.

ON THIS DAY, at _____ 10 a m _____ personally appeared

Edward Nason Master of the _Barque_ called the

Abbot Lord of _Boston_ Burthen per Register 437 Tons

laden with _a General Cargo_ bound from _Lpool_ _____

to _Boston_ _____ sailed the 26th Novr _____ and

arrived here _on the 15 of Decmr 1847_ and said Vessel having

experienced very severe weather and was obliged

to bear up for Cork. ———————————————

————————————————————————————————

————————————————————————————————

Desires to Note PROTEST, for all losses, costs, damages or delays suffered
r to be suffered, on account thereof.

MURPHY,
States Consul, COVE.

Signed
Edward Nason Master.

a true Copy

Note of Protest issued through U.S. Consul at Cork, Ireland, 15 December 1847. This document
established the right to formally protest a claim within a few days if necessary.

Protest executed through the U.S. Consul at Lisbon, (first page) 14 January 1811. *This document was often completely handwritten, but printed forms were used also. A typical protest might be two or three pages in length, almost always beginning with the phrase, "By this public Instrument of Protest..." Common dimensions might be 12 1/2" x 8", with little decorative engraving. Consular seals or customs and notary stamps will be found on some copies.*

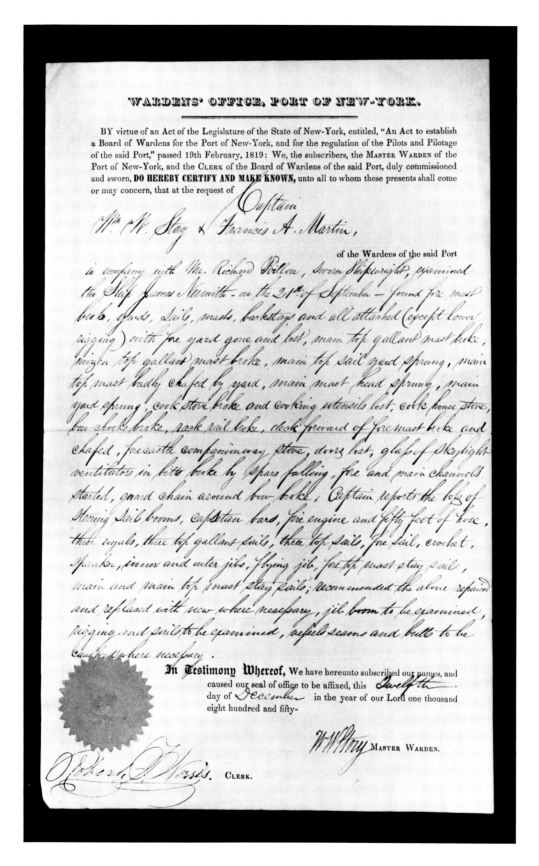

Survey Certificate, 12 December 1850, *on the vessel* James Nesmith, *signed by the Master Warden at the Port of New York. These certificates varied in content and style. Many were completely handwritten and signed by the surveyors. Some copies carried official stamps or seals.*

Notary document appointing two shipmasters and a ship carpenter to survey the bark Abbot Lord, *"...having sprung a leak at sea and being under the necessity of putting into port for repairs..." 4 June 1846.*

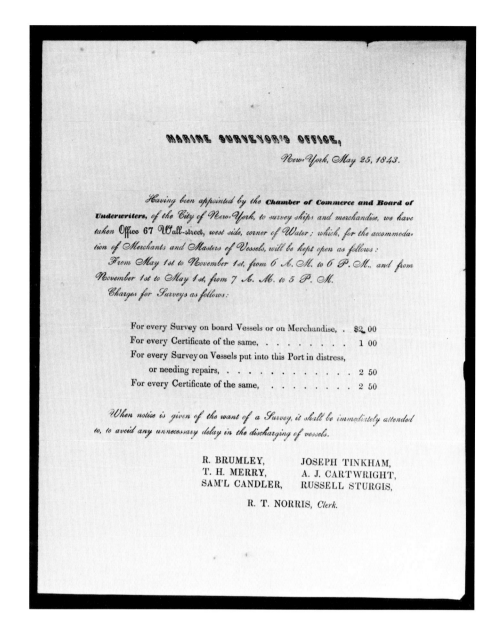

MARINE SURVEYOR'S OFFICE,

New-York, May 25, 1843.

Having been appointed by the **Chamber of Commerce and Board of Underwriters**, of the City of New-York, to survey ships and merchandise, we have taken Office 67 Wall-street, west side, corner of Water; which, for the accommodation of Merchants and Masters of Vessels, will be kept open as follows:

From May 1st to November 1st, from 6 A. M. to 6 P. M., and from November 1st to May 1st, from 7 A. M. to 5 P. M.

Charges for Surveys as follows:

For every Survey on board Vessels or on Merchandise, . . $2 00
For every Certificate of the same, ... 1 00
For every Survey on Vessels put into this Port in distress,
    or needing repairs, ... 2 50
For every Certificate of the same, ... 2 50

When notice is given of the want of a Survey, it shall be immediately attended to, to avoid any unnecessary delay in the discharging of vessels.

R. BRUMLEY,   JOSEPH TINKHAM,
T. H. MERRY,   A. J. CARTWRIGHT,
SAM'L CANDLER,   RUSSELL STURGIS,

R. T. NORRIS, *Clerk.*

The Marine Surveyor's notice above indicates that they were appointed by the Chamber of Commerce and Board of Underwriters of the City of New York. Their services and related charges are prominently advertised, 25 May 1843.

Bottomry Bond. Sold by Negbaur & Co., Stationers, Montgomery-St. San Francisco, Cal.

Original

Know all Men by these Presents, THAT

I, H. H. Hobbs now Master and Commander of the Ship or vessel called the Morning Glory of the burthen of Eleven hundred & fourteen tons, or thereabouts, now lying in the port of Port Townsend am held and firmly bound unto

S. B. Ivelan

in the sum of Nine thousand Six hundred & ninety two 76/100 dolls lawful money of the United States of America, to be paid to the said S. B. Ivelan or to his certain *Attorney* executors, administrators or assigns: for which payment well and truly to be made, I bind myself, my heirs, executors and administrators, and also the said vessel, her tackle, apparel and furniture, firmly by these Presents. Sealed with my seal, at Port Townsend this twenty Sixth day of Sept in the year of our Lord one thousand eight hundred and fifty nine

Whereas the above bounden H. H. Hobbs has been obliged to take up and borrow, and hath received of the said S. B. Ivelan for the use of the said vessel, and for the purpose of fitting the same for sea, the sum of four thousand eight hundred & forty Six 38/100 dollars lawful money of the United States of America, which sum is to be and remain as a lien and bottomry on the said vessel, her tackle, apparel and furniture, and the cargo laden on board

at the rate or premium of twenty five per centum for the voyage. In consideration whereof, all risks of the seas, rivers, enemies, fires, pirates, &c., are to be on account of the said lender And for the better security of the said sum and premium, the said master doth, by these presents, hypothecate and assign over to the said S. B. Ivelan his heirs, executors, administrators and assigns, the said vessel, her tackle, apparel and furniture, And it is hereby declared, that the said vessel, & Cargo is thus hypothecated and assigned over for the security of the money so borrowed, and taken up as aforesaid, and shall be delivered for no other use or purpose whatever, until this Bond is first paid, together with the premium hereby agreed to be paid thereon.

Now the Condition of this Obligation is such, That if the above bounden H. H. Hobbs shall well and truly pay or cause to be paid, unto the said

S. B. Ivelan

the just and full sum of lawful money as aforesaid, being the sum borrowed, and also the premium aforesaid, at or before the expiration of ten days after the arrival of the said vessel at

the port of San Francisco

then this obligation, and the said hypothecation, to be void and of no effect, otherwise to remain in full force and virtue. Having signed and executed three Bonds of the same tenor and date, one of which being accomplished, the others to be void and of no effect.

Signed, sealed and delivered in the presence of

Jno. Cbarson

W. H. Frost

H H Hobbs

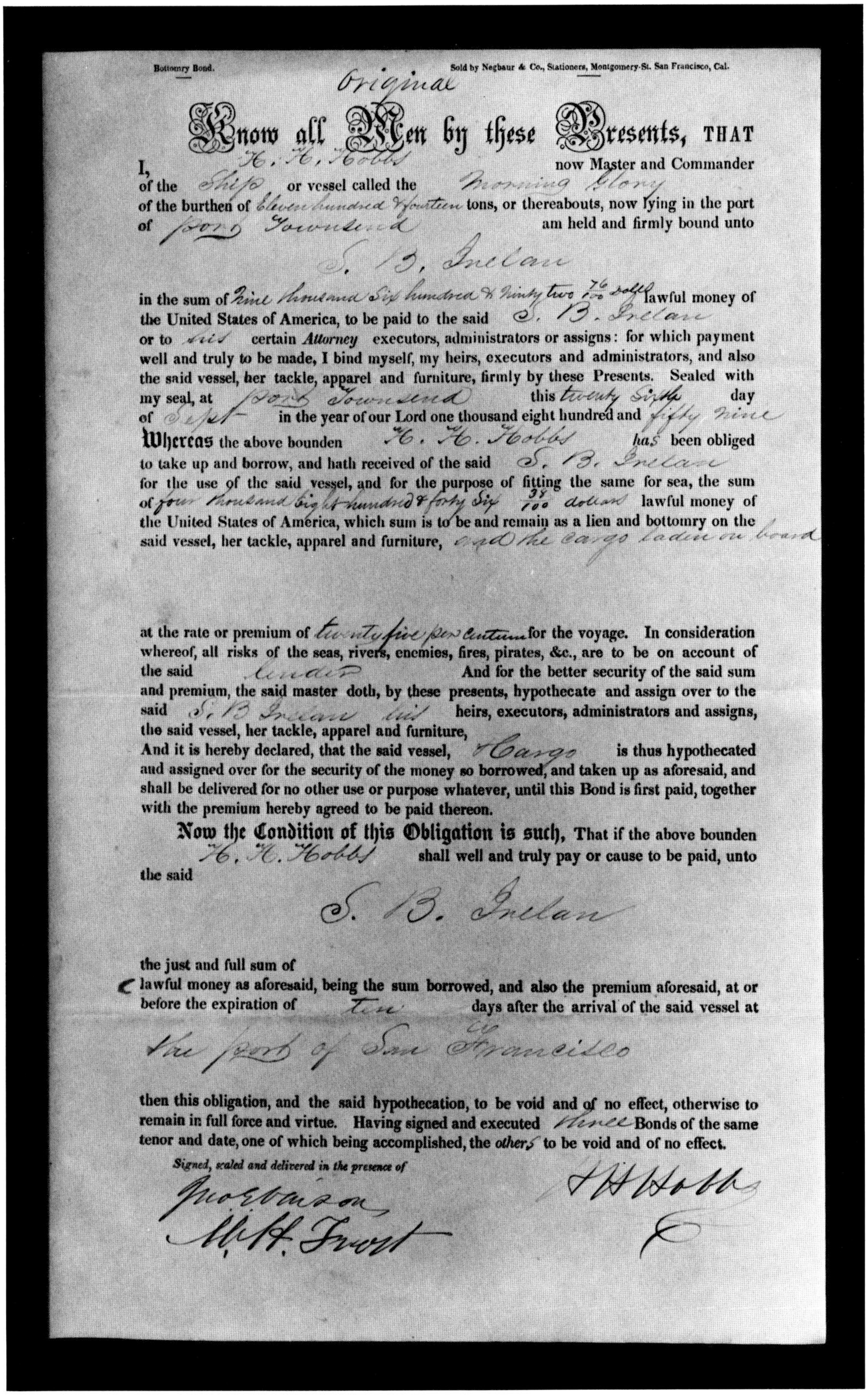

Bottomry Bond *indicating that the master of the ship* Morning Glory *borrowed $9,692.76 at 25% interest in Port Townsend, Washington, 26 September 1859. These documents were frequently handwritten and executed before a notary, consul, or customs official. Many were more detailed than the one shown above, and would often contain several pages. There was little standardization in size or style, but 12 1/2"x 8" was a common measurement.*

AVERAGE BOND.

Whereas the *Ship Morning Glory of Portsmouth* whereof *H. H. Hobbs* is *Master*, having on board a cargo of merchandise, sailed from the port of *Port Townsend* on the *29* day of *May* 1859 bound for *Iquique* and *Callao* and in the due prosecution of her said voyage, *struck upon Race Rocks in the Straits of San Juan de Fuca, became water logged, and was run on the beach at Esquimault V. I. thence after the employment of a Steam pump was put to sea and again compelled to return to Port Townsend and underwent temporary repairs in the Sound to enable her to reach San Francisco to go upon a dock, where she was permanently repaired after discharge of Cargo, &c &c, full particulars of which will appear in the accompanying documents* by which means certain losses and expenses have been incurred, and other expenses hereafter may be incurred, in consequence thereof, which, (according to the usage of this port,) constitute a General Average, to be apportioned on the said vessel, her earnings as freight and the Cargo on board.

Now we, the subscribers, owners, shippers, consignees, agents, or attorneys of certain consignees of said Vessel or Cargo, do hereby, for ourselves, our executors, and administrators, severally and respectively, but not jointly, or one for the other, covenant and agree to and with

H. H. Hobbs.

that the loss and damages aforesaid and other incidental expenses thereon, as shall be made to appear to be due from us, the subscribers to these presents, either as owners, shippers, consignees, agents or attorneys of certain consignees of said Vessel or Cargo, shall be paid by us, respectively, according to our parts, or shares in the said Vessel, her earnings as Freight, and her said Cargo, as shall belong, or be consigned to us, or shall belong, or be consigned to any person or persons with whom we are co-partners, agents, or attorneys, or in any manner concerned therein, provided such losses, and expenses aforementioned to be stated and apportioned by *I. P. Haven,* Average Adjuster in accordance with established usages and laws of this State in similar cases. And for the faithful performance of all and singular in the premises, we do severally hereby bind ourselves, our respective heirs, executors and administrators to the said

H. H. Hobbs

This Average Bond indicated *that damage had occurred during a voyage by the* Morning Glory *which constituted a General Average. The master, H.H. Hobbs, is guaranteeing that everyone involved in the loss will stand by their obligations under the principle of general average, 29 May 1859.*

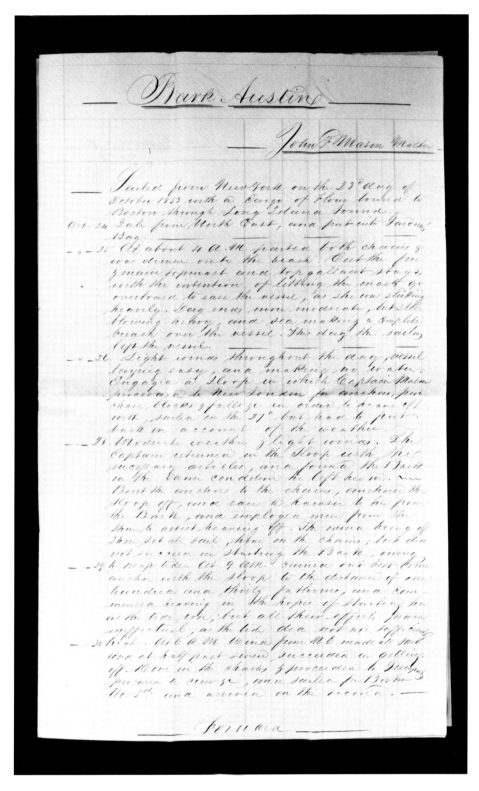

General Average Statement (4 pages). *First page describes storm damage to bark* Austin *during a passage from New York to Boston 24-30 October 1853. The remaining three pages contain a complete and final accounting of the average which totaled $766.70. The amount assigned to the General Average was $396.28. This document was completed by the insurance brokers in Boston and dated 25 February 1854, four months after the loss occurred. These statements often included an accounting of Particular Average; and "partial loss." They were always handwritten business documents with no seals or stamps in evidence.*

Bark Austin

Total — Disbursements &c. — | General Aver | Owners

	Labor employed from the shore to assist in getting vessel off			
9	Albert B. Edwards, labor agent getting vessel off	9	
9	S. M. Edwards — do —	9	
9	Thompson King — do —	9	
6	Thomas I. Davis — do —	6	
25	Josiah Miller, R. King, A. M. King, John Tudor, V. Jos... @ 5 each do	25	
10	carrying men back to the Island	10	
	Wm M. Tuthill		
60	services rendered with Sloop Flying Cloud & crew proceeding to New London returning to assist, assistance heaving the Bark off &c &c	60	
3	Captain Mann Expences at New London	3	
12	Cash paid for boat hire when ashore, to bring Capt Pattison who was sent as agent from New London to the Bark	12	
143	Forward	143	

Page two of the General Average Statement listing charges to the general average and to the owners.

Page three of the General Average Statement *listing charges to the general average and to the owners.*

Page four of the General Average Statement *showing the final accounting for bark* Austin's *damage, between the general average (396.28) and the owners (370.42).*

MARINE SOCIETY MEMBERSHIP CERTIFICATE

Marine societies began to appear in America during the mid-eighteenth century, with the Boston Marine Society (1742) and the Salem Marine Society (1766) being among the oldest. By 1860 these organizations were prominent in many port cities of the United States. They were comprised of seamen or mariners who applied and met various requirements for membership. The primary objective was to provide relief and assistance for aged or disabled members and their families. Most societies, however, also sought to establish lighthouses and other navigational aids for their local waterways. In a broader context, Marine societies often promoted maritime education and safety, while extending economic or social assistance to their membership and their community.

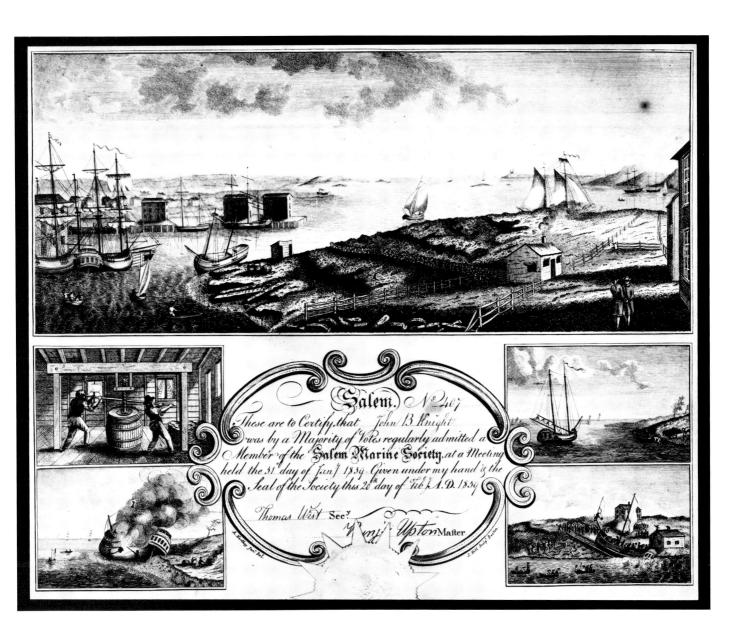

Membership Certificate No. 407, *from the Salem Marine Society to John B. Knight, 31 January 1839. Detailed nautical engravings frequently appear on these documents, in addition to the society's seal and the signatures of the appropriate officers. (Mss.Coll., Peabody Museum, Salem, MA . Photo by Mark Sexton.)*

Master Carpenter's Certificate

Usually a brief printed document, found in various sizes. The form often included the phrase, "__do certify that the___named the__was built by me or under my direction at__during the year__for__...." Title of the certificate and the port of issue was usually printed at the top. A rather plain document with little or no engraving. Stamps or seals seldom appear, and customs officials' signatures were not required.

This document was procured from the customhouse once the construction of a new vessel was finished. It was filled out and signed by the builder or carpenter, and contained spaces to record the vessel's name, measurements, the place and year of construction, and the names of the original owners. The vessel could then, if necessary, be moved from where it was built to where it was to be registered or sold. In fact this document was required before any registration or enrollment could be issued, since it established a ship's origin and ownership.

Measurement Certificate (Certificate of Admeasurement)

A printed document. Size and format may vary, but the title "(Certificate of Admeasurement)," and the issuing port's name is often printed near the top. Certificates are rather plain, with an absence of decorative engraving, stamps or seals. Many examples include the phrase, "I__being hereunto appointed by__ Collector of Customs for the District of__, do certify that I have surveyed and admeasured a__having the name of__..." The signature of the surveyor is usually present.

A measurement certificate officially established a vessel's tonnage and measurements. It provided the physical description needed in order to obtain a register or enrollment. A new measurement certificate was required whenever a vessel underwent some change in her measurement, rig, or other alteration that affected her tonnage, so that a revised registration could be issued to the vessel's owners. The document was filled in and signed by a qualified surveyor appointed by the customs collector. The measurement certificate was often reproduced as part of a vessel's Bill of Sale, and the information recorded on other maritime documents like registers and enrollments.

(Certificate of Admeasurement.)

DISTRICT OF NEW BEDFORD.

Port of *Mattapoisett June 9th* 1853

I *Ansel Weeks* being hereunto appointed by *William T. Russell for* Collector of the Customs for the District of New Bedford, do certify, that I have surveyed and admeasured a *Ship* having the name of *Rein-Deer* of *New Bedford* painted on her stern according to law, and that said vessel is *Carvel* built, has *Two* decks *Three* mast *Square* stern with *no* tuck, has *no* gallery, and *a Billet* head, that she is in length *123* feet *6* inches, in breadth *28* feet *4* inches, and in depth *14* feet *2* inches, and that she measures *449* tons and *93* ninety-fifth parts of a ton. As witness my hand,

Countersigned in testimony of the truth of the particulars above mentioned, by

Septr 16th 9w

Ansel Weeks

(Master Carpenter's Certificate.)

DISTRICT OF NEW BEDFORD.

Port of *Mattapoisett Septr 9* 1853

We *Josiah Holmes & Bro.* of *Mattapoisett* do certify that the *Ship* named the *Reindeer* was built by us or under our direction at *Mattapoisett* during the *Years 1852 & 1853* for *Edward W Howland one Quarter, Cornelius Howland seven thirty-seconds, B Franklin Howland one eighth, Oliver Crocker one sixteenth George C Crocker one sixteenth, George Barney one sixteenth Charles R Tucker one thirty second, Edward D Mandell one thirty second all of New Bedford county of Bristol and State of Massachusetts and Lorenzo Smith one sixteenth & Peter Crowell one sixteenth both of Tisbury county of Dukes & State aforesaid and Josiah Holmes one sixteenth & H Holmes one sixteenth both of Mattapoisett county of Plymouth* that said *Ship* is *Carvel* built; has *two* decks *& three & state aforesaid*

Three mast *S* *123* feet *6* inches in length, *28* feet *4* inches in breadth, *14* feet *2* inches in depth, of *449* $\frac{93}{95}$ tons burthen. As witness my hand the day and year aforesaid.

Josiah Holmes & Bro.

A *Master Carpenter's Certificate and Certificate of Admeasurement* were often printed on a single document. Illustrated is a certificate executed at Mattapoisett, Massachusetts for the new ship Reindeer, *June 6, 1853.*

    Printed document, approximately 6¼" x 11", enclosed by 1/4" embellished border. "American Ship Masters' Association" is engraved on the upper portion of the certificate. Below is an engraving of a full-rigged ship, on the left side of which is the number of the certificate and on the right side of which is engraved "New York," home of the Association and site of the 1861 examinations. The signature of the certificate holder was required, as were the signatures of various members of the society. The engravings and ornamentation varied throughout the years that these Certificates were issued.

    The American Shipmasters' Association, later the American Bureau of Shipping, was organized in 1861 to improve the American Mercantile Marine Service and the general skill and moral character of those attached to the seamen's profession. Licenses had been issued intermittently by the United States Steamboat Inspection Service, but no continuous effort had been made to insure the skill and character of shipmasters until John D. Jones called together maritime insurers, shipbuilders, government officials and maritime experts to form the American Shipmasters' Association in 1861. The ASA began issuing certificates to qualified mates and masters of sailing vessels even before its incorporation in 1862, receiving the first application from Captain Isaiah Pratt in September, 1861. To receive a certificate, seamen had to meet rigorous requirements, including six years experience at sea and a high score on the nautical science and seamanship examinations administered by the ASA. Applicants also had to produce testimonials to their good character. Shipmasters whose qualifications were exceptional were designated "extra masters." Each certificate was valid for one year and could be renewed annually. Seamen retained their ASA numbers for life; no number was ever reissued to another man. While ASA certificates were not officially required of shipmasters, they did serve as recommendations to shipowners. A vessel with an ASA-certified master was more likely to find favorable insurance coverage than one whose master was not listed in the ASA's Register of Approved Shipmasters. The ASA continued its program of certification until 1900, by which time Federal law required that most shipmasters be licensed by the United States.

The Mediterranean Passport, commonly called a ship's passport, was created after the United States concluded a treaty with Algiers in 1795. During the early years of independence, America was one of several nations paying tribute to the Barbary states in exchange for the ability to sail and conduct business in the Mediterranean area without interference. This treaty provided American-owned vessels with a "Passport" that would be recognized by Algeria and later by other Barbary states through similar treaties. These Passports were to be issued only to vessels that were completely owned by citizens of the United States, and were intended to serve as additional evidence of official nationality.

In June 1796, a Federal law was passed which required the Secretary of State to prepare a form for the Passport and submit it to the President for approval. The result was a document modeled after a similar British form, called a Mediterranean Pass, which England had employed for the same purpose. The American version was a printed document, on vellum, that measured approximately 15" x 11." Centered in the upper half were two engravings, one below the other, (some early examples had a single large engraving of a lighthouse with a ship at anchor across the entire top quarter of the document). Signatures of the President of the United States, Secretary of State, and Customs Collector appear in the lower right-hand corner. The United States seal is in the lower left-hand corner.

The most obvious similarity with the British passport was the presence of a scalloped line of indenture across the upper part of the document which was used a a method of authentication. After they were printed, the Passports were cut along the waved line and the top portion sent to the U.S. Consuls along the Barbary coast. The Consuls subsequently provided copies to the corsairs, whose commanders were instructed to let all vessels proceed, who had passes that fit the scalloped tops.

Every American vessel sailing in this area was to have a Mediterranean Passport as part of its papers. The penalty for sailing without one was $200.00. The master requested the document from the collector and paid a fee of ten dollars. A bond was also required to insure that the Passport was used in accordance with the conditions under which it was obtained, and was canceled when the document was forfeited. New Passports were not required for each succeeding foreign voyage, but it could not be transferred to another vessel, and it was to be returned to the port of original issue if the ship was wrecked or sold.

Mediterranean Passports were received by the various customs districts pre-signed by the President and Secretary of State. The Collector could then insert the vessel's name and tonnage, master's name, number of crew members, and the number of guns mounted on the vessel, into the appropriate blanks and sign the document. It is interesting to note that I have found one Passport issued and dated nearly six months after the President whose signature appears on the document had left office. One might wonder just how efficiently these rather important forms were managed. Unused and outdated Passports were supposed to be returned to the Treasury Department, after first being canceled by cutting holes through the seals.

Unlike the Mediterranean Passport, the Sea Letter does not appear to have had any formal establishment, but rather acquired validity through years of maritime use. The term "Sea Letter" has been used to describe any document issued by a government or monarch to one of its merchant fleet, which established proof of nationality and guaranteed protection for the vessel and her owners. However, it is the Sea Letter used by the United States after 1789 that is of particular interest here.

MEDITERRANEAN PASSPORT/SEA LETTER

The 1822 edition of *The Merchants and Shipmaster's Assistant* described the Sea Letter as a document which "specifies the nature of the cargo and the place of destination," and says that it was only required for vessels bound to the Southern Hemisphere. It further indicated that "...this paper is not so necessary as the passport, because that, in most particulars, supplies its place." In 1859 the document was defined as part of the ship's papers when bound on a foreign voyage, "...it is written in four languages, the French, Spanish, English, and Dutch, and is only necessary for vessels bound round Cape Horn and the Cape of Good Hope."

Like the Mediterranean Passport, the Sea Letter was a remarkably standardized document which changed little during the time that it was used. Usually printed on heavy grade paper, approximately 16" x 20" in size, the first Sea Letters carried only three languages instead of four. However, they soon became known as "Four Language Sea Letters."

The statement within the document conveys in part that the vessel described is owned entirely by American citizens, and requests that all "Prudent Lords, Kings, Republics, Princes, Dukes, Earls, Barons, Lords, Burgomasters, Schepens, Consullors..." etc., treat the vessel and her crew with fairness and respect. The signatures of the President of the United States, the Secretary of State, and the customs collector appear, usually in the middle portion of the document. The United States seal is present, while customs and consular stamps or seals are frequently in evidence.

Sea Letters are mentioned in the formative maritime legislation forged by the new Federal government. Like passports, they provided additional evidence of ownership and nationality, but the criteria by which a shipmaster utilized one document over the other is not completely clear. It was explained at the time that both documents were "rendered necessary or expedient by reason of treaties with foreign powers," a statement which suggests that certain nations required a particular document because of existing agreements with the United States.

In any case the Sea Letter was valid for only a single voyage, and a bond does not seem to have been required. Neither was it to be returned to the collector when the voyage was completed. Indications are that, as the years progressed, Sea Letters were being used more often by whaling ships than by merchant vessels, perhaps because American whalers fished in areas where this document was preferred as proof of national origin.

By providing a statement of American property, signed by the President of the United States, the Mediterranean Passport and the Sea Letter were intended to confirm our status as a neutral nation, when international conflict put added dangers on America's commerce at sea. By mid-century, however, much of what had previously threatened our shipping was being neutralized by the expanding power of the United States. In 1831 Congress eliminated the fee required for obtaining a Mediterranean Passport. It was argued at the time that the revenue arising from that source, and the protection which it provided, were no longer objects of any importance. As our merchant fleet became more secure, fewer shipowners and shipmasters considered these documents as necessary to guarantee their rights and safety in foreign lands.*

Both pieces were considered important parts of a ship's papers in the 1800s. They were kept aboard ship during the voyage and deposited, along with the Registry Certificate, with the appropriate U.S. consular authority anytime the vessel was in a foreign port. The Mediterranean Passport had disappeared from use by 1860, while the Sea Letter was still in evidence several years later.

Today both pieces are considered to be important documents in any maritime collection. However, they are also highly valued by autograph collectors and investors, which keeps many fine pieces in private hands.

It is important here to note that both documents were intended only to protect the vessel from capture or destruction by proving American, – i.e., nonbelligerent – ownership. American crew members aboard these ships were still vulnerable to impressment, especially if they did not carry their own personal protection certificate as proof of citizenship.

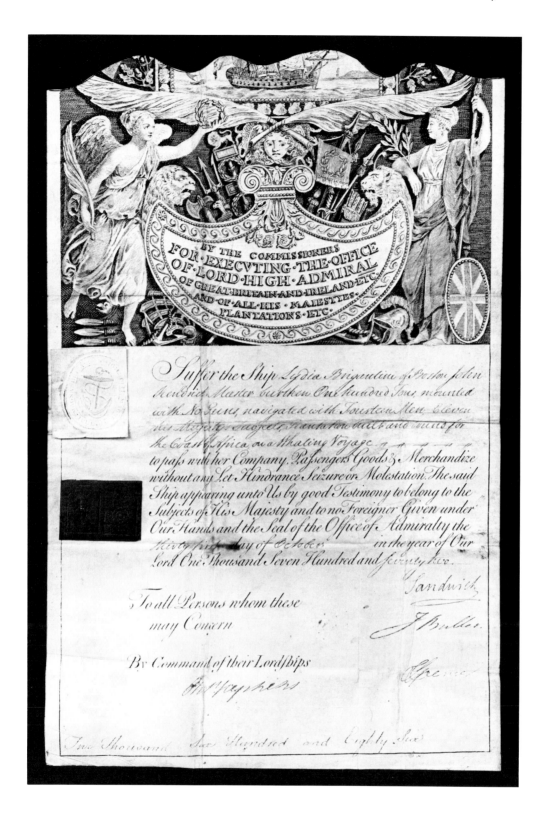

The United States modeled the ship's Passport *after a similar British document known as a Mediterranean Pass, shown above. This particular document was issued by the Admiralty to the Brigantine* Lydia *for a whaling voyage from Boston to the African coast, 31 October 1772. Admiralty seal and revenue stamps are present along the left-hand edge. Like its American counterpart, the Mediterranean Pass was printed on vellum, and is similar in dimensions and style.*

A typical Mediterranean Passport issued to the ship Canton Packet *from the collector at the district of Bristol & Warren, Rhode Island, on 1 November 1832. Signed by President Andrew Jackson, and Edward Livingston, Secretary of State. The number "5" written above the seal indicates that this was the fifth Passport issued there during that year. This figure can provide valuable information as to the number of Passports issued at various ports, and how it was affected by perceived threats to American shipping during periods of international conflict.*

KNOW all Men by these Presents, That we *Geo. A. Hallowell, Mariner, and Thomas P. Ives, Merchant, both of Providence in the State of Rhode-Island &c.*

are held and firmly bound to the present Treasurer of the United States of America, and to his Successor in Office, in Trust for the said United States, in the just and full Sum of Two Thousand Dollars, Money of the said United States, to which Payment well and truly to be made, we bind Ourselves, our Heirs, Executors and Administrators, jointly and severally by these Presents. Witness our Hands and Seals, this *Seventh* Day of *December* Eighteen Hundred and *Seven*.

The Condition of this Obligation is such, That whereas JEREMIAH OLNEY, Collector of the Customs for the District of PROVIDENCE, has this Day issued and granted a Passport, numbered *129,* pursuant to the Act, entitled "An Act providing Passports for the Ships and Vessels of the United States," for the *Brigantine* called *Argus,* of the Burthen of *One Hundred and Five* Tons, or thereabouts, mounted with *two* Guns, navigated with *Eight* Men, of which the above named *Geo. H. Hallowell* is at present Master; the said *Brigantine* being a Vessel of the United States of America, as appears by her Certificate of Registry, now presented, which Certificate was granted at *Providence* in the District of *Providence* on the *Fourth* Day of *Decr instant,* and numbered *47.*

NOW THEREFORE, if the said Passport shall not be applied to the Use or protection of any other Vessel than the one described in the same, and in Case of the Loss or Sale of the said *Brigantine* at any Place within the United States, if the said Passport shall be delivered up to the Collector of the Customs for the said District of PROVIDENCE, within three Months after such Loss or Sale shall happen; or, if the said Passport shall be delivered up as aforesaid within six Months, if such Loss or Sale shall happen beyond the Limits of the United States, and nearer than the Cape of Good Hope; or within eighteen Months, if such Loss or Sale shall happen at any Place more distant than the said Cape of Good Hope; then, the above Obligation, shall be Void, and of no Effect; otherwise, it shall remain in full Force and Virtue.

Signed, Sealed and Delivered,
in Presence of
Geo. Olney

Geo. A. Hallowell

Tho. P. Ives

A $2,000 Bond signed by the master, and the agent or owner of the brigantine Argus. *Issued at the Providence customs district, it pledged compliance with the conditions under which they have obtained their vessel's Passport. The document was issued on 7 December 1807, three days after the applicants had received the passport. (Courtesy of Rhode Island Historical Society.)*

MEDITERRANEAN PASSPORT/SEA LETTER

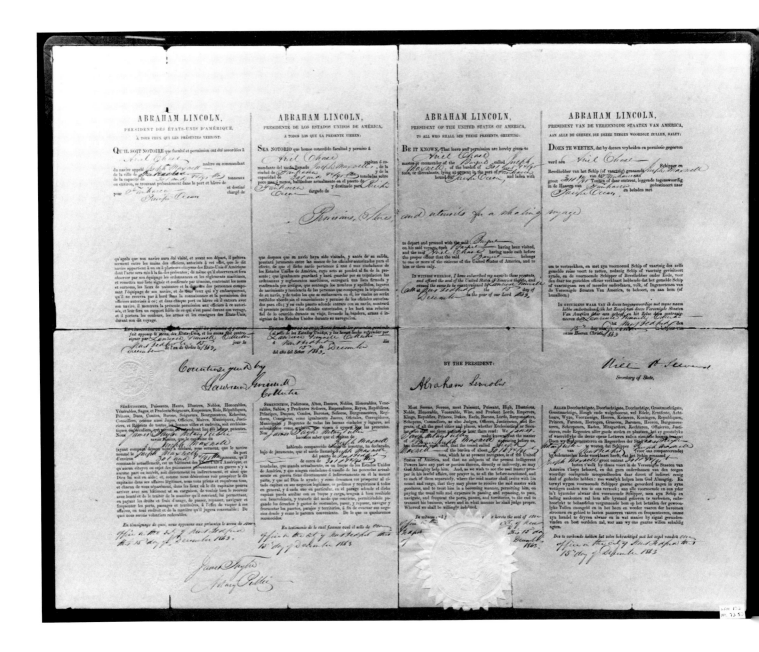

This Four-Language Sea Letter was issued to the whaling bark Joseph Maxwell *of Fairhaven, Massachusetts, 15 December 1863. Unlike the Mediterranean Passport, the Sea Letter required the signature of a notary official to whom the master had given a sworn oath of accuracy regarding the information on the document. This example bears the signatures of President Abraham Lincoln and Secretary of State William P. Seward at right, and the great seal at the bottom.*

Oaths of various kinds often appear in maritime collections, and are especially common in papers that were created during the early years of the nineteenth century. The concept or practice of oaths is not unique to maritime matters, but they were frequently required by customs, consular, or other authorities to help establish compliance with the numerous regulations and procedures that governed America's maritime trade. The language used on these forms remained fairly consistent throughout this period. They exist as separate documents, and are also printed on Manifests, Crew Lists, or other papers for which a particular oath was required. A sample of the variety of Oath forms are represented here.

Master's Oath on entering Vessel: *Customs form, signed by the shipmaster, wherein he swears that the manifest and other papers relative to his vessel's cargo is accurate in every respect, New York, 5 May 1804. This document was executed after a vessel entered port and the master was filing his cargo manifest with the customs authorities. Signatures of the deputy collector and naval officer also appear.*

Customs Oaths of Compliance, July 1813, *typical of those required by the local districts during the early nineteenth century. In this example, the shipmaster, upon arrival, signs sworn statements that he has delivered all appropriate mail to the post office, that his cargo manifest is accurate, and that to his knowledge there are no illegal goods aboard the brig. Ten days later, before departing, he swears to the accuracy of the ship's register, and confirms that the vessel is completely owned by American citizens. This particular document was evidently a copy of the various originals, and was given to the shipmaster for his records.*

2.

FORM of the OATH of an Owner or Owners of Goods, who may be
Manufacturer or Manufacturers in whole or in part of the same.

ST. CROIX, } to wit.

I[1] *Anthony John Hill* — of[2] *St Croix*
Merchant —
solemnly, sincerely, and truly[3] *Swear* that[4] *I am*
doing business at[5] *St Croix*
under the firm of[6] *Anthony John Hill & Co and*

for anyt of Messenger Estate Savain the true and lawful[7] *owners*
of certain Goods, Wares, or Merchandise, as specified in the Invoice subscribed
by the proper Signature of[8] *Anthony John Hill & Co*
amounting to[9] *Seven Hundred Seventy Dollars and
Sixty four cents*

and here produced to[10] *me Joseph Ridgway Consul
of The United States of America at the Island
of St Croix* ——— and[11] ——— shipped
at St. Croix, by[12] *Anthony John Hill & Co* ———
for[13] *Philadelphia* ——— in the United States
of America : that the said Invoice, hereunto annexed, contains a true and faithful
Account of the said **Goods, Wares,** or **Merchandise,** at the fair market value at the
time and place when and where the same were manufactured, and of all **Charges**
thereon ; and that the said Invoice contains no **Discounts, Bounties,** or **Drawbacks,**
but such as have been actually allowed.

*Given from under my
Hand and seat of my
Office at the Island
Aforesaid this fourteenth
Day of June and year
One thousand Eight
Hundred and thirty four*

Joseph Ridgway

**Directions for filling up
the Blanks.**

1. Deponent's name.
2. Place of residence, and profession.
3. "Sworn," or (if of the Society of Friends, called Quakers,) "affirm."
4. "I," or (if in partnership), "I and my partner," or "partners."
5. The place where established in business.
6. The firm.
7. "Owner," or "Owners."
8. "Myself," or "the firm."
9. Total value in pounds, shillings and pence, in words at length.
10. The name of the Mayor, Magistrate, Notary, or Master in Chancery, before whom sworn, with the place where he may act.
11. If not shipped, "intended to be."
12. Name of the shipper.
13. The port of destination.

**Directions for Signing and
Certifying the INVOICE.**

Each invoice must be signed either by the Firm of which the Deponent is partner, or by the Deponent himself, before he sign the affidavit, It also is requisite that the Magistrate, Notary, or Master in Chancery, administering the oath, certify thus on each invoice, viz.

" This is the Invoice referred to in the Affidavit of ———

" Sworn before me, this ——— day of ———, 18 ." In the }

In case the owner be of the Society of Friends (called Quakers,) read "affirmant," instead of "deponent," and "affirmation," instead of "oath."; "affidavit," or "oath."

** **Pray take Notice,** that this Verification, with the Invoice, must be certified by the Consul of the United States, without
which it will not be admitted in the said States.

*Oath of an Owner or Owners of Goods who may be manufacturers in whole or in part of
the same. This consular form indicates that the goods, valued at $770.64, are owned by the depo-
nent, and are being shipped by him to the United States. Document contains the signature of the U.S.
Consul, and the consular seal, St. Croix, 14 June 1834. These forms were often attached to the
appropriate invoice or vessel's cargo manifest.*

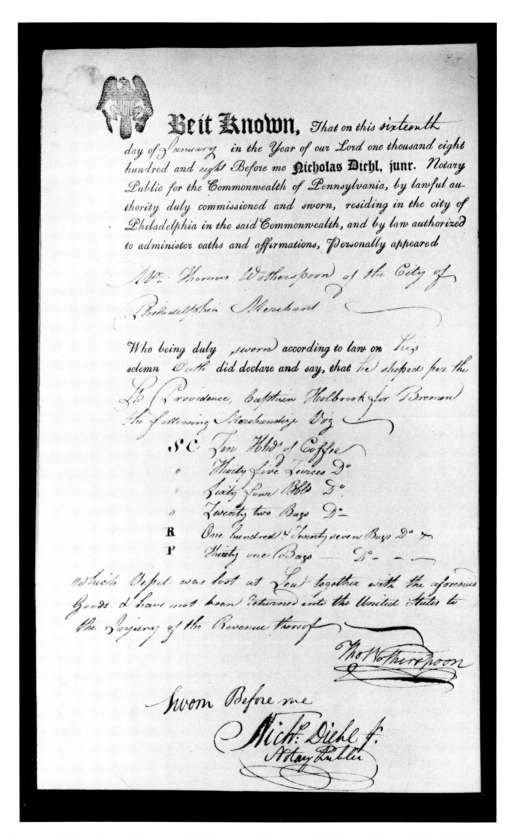

Oath regarding loss of cargo: *This notary document indicates that a Philadelphia merchant swears to the loss of his shipment of coffee when the vessel carrying his cargo to Bremen was lost at sea, Philadelphia 16 January 1808. This form would have been part of the process necessary for the shipper to file a claim against those who had insured his cargo. Contains notary stamp, and the signatures of the deponent and the Notary Public.*

Upon entering an American port from a foreign country, the shipmaster, in accordance with the 1819 "Act Regulating Passenger Ships and Vessels," filed a list of passengers with the customs officer, and swore to the accuracy of its contents, in the same manner as required for a cargo manifest. The list contained information about the voyage, including the vessel and master's names, port of embarkation and arrival, and the date of arrival. Passenger information required name, age, sex, occupation, country of origin, destination, and circumstances of death during the voyage when applicable. Similar information was recorded for tourists and American citizens as well. As immigration increased, legislation was enacted that required more data about each passenger, such as proficiency in languages and last legal residence. The customs collector was also required to prepare copies and abstracts of the passenger lists for quarterly reports to the State Department, in accordance with the Act of 1819. Passenger lists could vary in size and format, especially during the first half of the nineteenth century. In addition, other unofficial lists of passengers are sometimes found in ship's logbooks, and in various kinds of maritime business or family papers. They usually prove to be a valuable source of research for the maritime historian or genealogist.

PASSENGER LIST

List or Manifest of all Passengers taken on board the *Ship Chelsea at London & Cowes* _____ *Acors Barns* _____ is Master, from *London* _____ Burthen 396 ³/₉₅ . . . . whereof Tons

NAMES.	AGE. Years	Months	SEX.	OCCUPATION.	The Country to which they severally belong.	The Country to which they intend to become inhabitants.	Died on the Voyage.
John Sabman —	61	6	Male	Gent —	England	Kentucky .	2 packages
Joseph Westbeach $450	23	2	do	do	Philadelphia	Phil'a	
Richard Hay — $1.5	24	11	do	do	— do —	Utica N.Y.	
Alexander Hart & family	51	9	do	Sales Smith	England —	New York	21 packages
Elizabeth do	51	6	Female	do	do	do do	
Hannah do	22	9	do		do	do do	
Julia do	25	7	do		do	do do	
Bloomy do Jn	16	6	do		do	do do	
Amelia do	14	6	do		do	do do	
Henry do	19		male	do do	do	do do	
Isaac do	12	6	do	do do	do	do do	
Jacob do	8	9	do	do do	do	do do	
Thomas Bran & family	43	6	do	Farmer	do —	Athens N.Y.	7 package
Philadelphia do	33	11	Female	do	do	do do —	died May 3
Abigal do	12	—	do	do	do	do do	
Louiza do $411	3	—	do	do	do	do do	
Susannah do	1	—	do	do	do	do do	
David do	18	—	male	do	do	do do	
Thomas do	14	—	do	do	do	do do	
Richard do	9	—	do	do	do	do do	
John Butcher $2	26	1	do	Sailor	do	Albany N.Y.	2 do
Maria do	23	—	Female		do	do do	
Davies John $6	36	1	male	Farmer —	do	do do	3 do
do Jane	32	—	Female	do do	do	do do	
„ William	12	—	male	do do	do	do do	
„ Thomas	10	—	do	do	do	do do	
„ John	8	—	do	do	do	do do	
„ Samuel	6	2	do	do	do	do do	
Mercer John & family	29	—	do	Farmer	do	Smith county	5 do

Portion of a single sheet Passenger List for the ship Chelsea, *London to New York, 1828.*

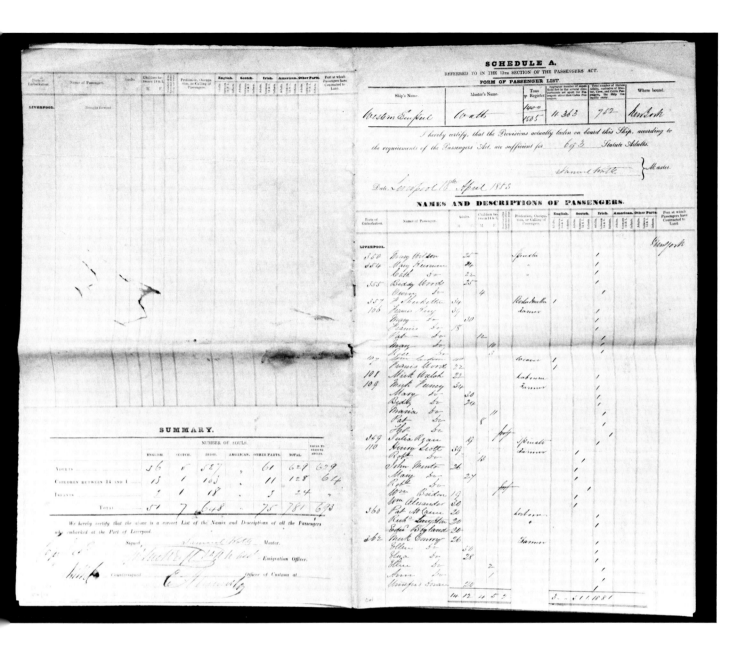

Front and back covers for a Passenger List, 1853, *containing several pages of information on 781 passengers aboard ship* Western Empire, *from Liverpool to New York.*

PILOT'S LICENSE (SAIL)

A one-page document, varying in size and style, usually with the name of the state or port under whose authority the license was granted, prominently written or printed near the top. Some early documents are completely hand written. Signatures of local commissioners, board members, or other officials responsible for examining and licensing the applicant will usually appear at the end of the document. Seals or notary stamps might also be found on some examples.

Pilots are responsible for the safe navigation of vessels up rivers, into harbors, and out again to the open sea. During the first half of the nineteenth century, pilots received their certification through the state within which the harbor was located. The states had the power to require pilotage in and out of their ports, and in the absence of any Federal legislation they provided their own regulations for pilots. This was often conducted by a state-appointed board of examiners, or commissioners, who handled the examinations and licensing of the pilot applicants, as well as the licensing of pilot boats.

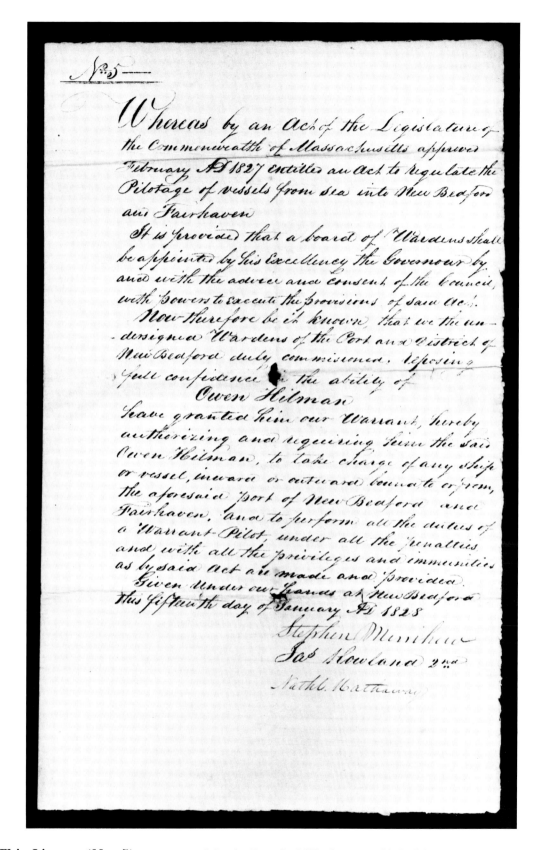

This License (No. 5) *was granted by the Board of Wardens, established by Massachusetts State law, to Owen Hilman, 15 January 1828. It authorized him "to take charge of any ship or vessel, inward or outward bound, to or from the aforesaid port of New Bedford and Fairhaven, and to perform all duties of a Warrant Pilot…"*

No. 32

State of Maryland,

CITY OF BALTIMORE.

In Pursuance of an *Act of Assembly of the State of Maryland*, passed January session, eighteen hundred and fifty-three, entitled "An Act to regulate Pilots,"

Permission is hereby Granted, by the BOARD OF PILOTS to the Master of the *Schooner* called the *Ocean Bird* of *Kingston* of the burthen of — — — — — 114 tons, to navigate the Chesapeake Bay, in said *Schooner* for twelve months, from the *Second* day of *Febuary* eighteen hundred and sixty

Witness the Seal of the BOARD OF EXAMINERS, countersigned by order of the Board, the *Second* day of *Febuary* eighteen hundred and sixty

John H. Cooper President.

114 Tons, at six cents per ton, $ 6.84
50 Seal
$7.34

CLIPPER PRINT.

This is a Pilot Boat License (No. 32) *granted by the Maryland Board of Pilots to the Master of the* Ocean Bird, *and effective for 12 months from 2 February 1860.*

ABSTRACT OF AN ACT

In addition to an Act to establish Regulations concerning the Harbor of Boston.

Be it enacted by the Senate and House of Representatives in General Court assembled, and by the authority of the same, as follows:

SECTION 1. The Harbor Master, authorized to be appointed by the fifth section of the Act to which this is an addition, shall have authority to regulate the anchorage of all vessels in the upper harbor of Boston, and, when necessary, to order the removal of such vessels, and to cause the same to be removed in obedience to such order, at the expense of the master or owners thereof; and if any person shall obstruct said Harbor Master in the performance of any of his duties, as prescribed by this Act, or by the Act to which this is an addition, or shall neglect or refuse to obey any lawful order made by said Harbor Master, he shall be liable to a penalty not exceeding fifty dollars for each offence, to be recovered by indictment, for the use of the City of Boston.

Harbor Regulations of the Port of Boston.

SECTION 1. All vessels anchoring on the south side of the channel must anchor by the following marks, viz: the tall steeple in Hanover Street in range with the granite block on Long Wharf and below the range of India Wharf. On the North, by Long Island Light in range with the Half-Moon Battery on Governor's Island, and southeasterly of the range of the Grand Junction Wharves, East Boston. Small vessels will anchor inside the above range, in order that sufficient room may be given for larger vessels to anchor in the range.

SECT. 2. All vessels anchoring contrary to Section 1. must be hauled immediately to some wharf, or they will be moved at the vessel's expense.

SECT. 3. The master, commander, or owner of every vessel shall, as soon as practicable, after having hauled to the end of any wharf that extends to the channel of said harbor, cause her lower yards to be cockbilled, and her topsail yards to be braced fore and aft, and her jib-boom to be rigged in, and the yards and jib-boom shall be kept so arranged while such vessel lies at the end of the wharf, as aforesaid, and until she is preparing immediately to leave her berth.

SECT. 4. No person shall throw or deposit in said harbor, or any part thereof, any stones, gravel, ballast, cinders, ashes, dirt, mud, or other substances which may in any respect tend to injure the navigation thereof.

SECT. 5. No warp or line shall be passed across the mouth of any slip, for the purpose of hauling any vessel by said slip, before the vessel shall be within one hundred feet of said slip, if the owners or occupants thereof object, unless the Harbor Master may think it necessary.

SECT. 6. All vessels at anchor in the harbor of Boston shall keep an anchor watch at all times, and shall keep a clear and distinct light suspended at least six feet above the deck during the night; and whenever the provisions of this section shall be violated on board any vessel, the master or owners shall be liable to a penalty of not more than twenty dollars, to be recovered in the manner provided in the Act to which this is an addition, and shall be held liable to pay all damages that may be occasioned by such violations.

Under no circumstances whatever are vessels permitted to lie at anchor in the track of the Ferry Boats, or in Fore Point Channel.

PARTICULAR NOTICE.

The telegraph wire has been laid in the track of both of the East Boston Ferries, and vessels are requested to govern themselves accordingly.

JOHN T. GARDNER,
Harbor Master of the Port of Boston.

Office — South side of Old East Boston Ferry.
On Eastern Avenue Wharf.

HEALTH ESTABLISHMENT,

Staten-Island, May 1st, 1826.

RULES

To be observed on board of all vessels directed to ride at Quarantine.

1. Colours must be worn in the main shrouds of all vessels at Quarantine until the Commander shall be furnished with a Bill of Health.

2. All persons whatever belonging to a vessel at Quarantine, are strictly prohibited from going on shore, except at the Health-Office wharf, *unless by permission of the Health Officer.*

3. All persons whatever belonging to a vessel at Quarantine, are forbid to take on board with them any person who did not arrive in such vessel; and all passengers, or other persons, who live on shore, are also prohibited from going on board their own vessels, *except by permission of the Health Officer.*

4. All communication between vessels put under Quarantine is expressly prohibited.

5. No boat shall be permitted to come on shore without an officer in it, and only between sun-rising and sun-setting, unless in cases of distress or sickness; and all boats must be alongside, or on board, by sun-down. The bell on the Health-Office boat-house will be rung ten minutes before sun-down, to give notice for all boats to go off to their respective vessels.

6. On Sundays all boats must put off to their vessels by ten o'clock in the morning, when the bell will be rung to give such notice, and the boats must not come on shore again before six o'clock in the evening.

7. No boat or craft is permitted to go along side of a vessel at Quarantine, for any purpose whatsoever, *except the Master thereof shall have a written permit from the Health-Officer.*

8. Provisions and other necessaries intended to be sent on board of a vessel at Quarantine, must be embarked from the Health-Office wharf only, except the Health-Officer grants a special permit to proceed to any other wharf.

9. No rum or spirituous liquors shall be sent or taken on board of vessels at Quarantine, except by an *order* from the commander of the vessel, signed by the Health-Officer.

10. Commanders of vessels are accountable for all irregularities committed on board their respective vessels, and for the conduct of such of their people as they may send on shore; and if any person shall elope from their vessel, a report thereof must be immediately made to the Health-Officer.

11. Universal cleanliness must be constantly preserved on board.

12. Wind-sails must be constantly kept up in each hatchway, and trimmed to the wind; for every day they are neglected or omitted (*except on account of the weather or discharging the cargo*), as many additional days of Quarantine will be added.

13. The bilge-water must be completely pumped out at least twice a-day, and water from along side be put in the pump, or any other more effectual manner, until the water so pumped out shall be clear, and free from any offensive smell.

14. All foul wearing apparel and bed-clothes of the passengers must be washed within the Quarantine limits—and all wearing apparel and bed-clothes of the officers and seamen, must be washed and aired; the beds of seamen emptied, and the ticks washed, when the filling may be put in again, if it is in good condition.

15. The forecastles to be scrubbed, scraped, and then whitewashed throughout, except the floor.

16. All passengers who intend to live on shore, during their Quarantine, are required to report to the Health-Officer, at his office, where they reside, immediately after they have engaged their lodgings, and to answer to the roll called at their boarding-houses at nine A. M. at three and seven P. M. under the penalty of an additional day's Quarantine being added for every violation.

17. All infractions of the foregoing rules will be punished as the law directs.

JOHN T. HARRISON, *Health-Officer.*

Rules and Regulations *for the conduct of shipping were posted at all ports, and also given to shipmasters if necessary upon their arrival. Illustrated is a copy of the harbor regulations for the port of Boston, ca. 1850, and quarantine procedures for vessels calling at New York in 1826.*

PORTAGE BILL of the *Ship Joseph Walker* _____ **Master, from** *New York* **to** *Liverpool & Home to New York* 11/30 1852

NAMES.	Stations.	Dates of Entry.	Dates of Discharge.	Duration of Service. Months Days	Wages per month.	Whole Wages.	Amount paid at N. York	Amount paid at Liverpool	Hospital Money.	Balance due.	SIGNATURES.
Chas. F. Watt	1 Mate	Sept 17	Nov 30	2 13	50	121 66	30.00		1 30	70 16	
John Williams	2nd "	" 17		2 13	35	85 17 33	35		1 30	13 07	
Daniel Burnes	Steward	" 17		2 13	25	60 82 25	27 50	1 —	7 32	
Philip Williams	Cook	" 17		2 13	22	53 52 22	25	1 —	5 52	
Henry Howard	Overlooker of Bags	" 17		2 13	20	48 66	— —	25	1 —	22 66	
John Boring	Ordinary	" 17		2 13	13	31 62 13	13	1 —	4 62	
John Powers	Boatswain	Oct 27		1 3	20	22 —		20	4 75	1 25	
Wm. Turner	3rd Mate	" 27		1 3	25	27 50		10	75	16 75	—
F. Murray	Seaman	" 27		1 3	11.25	12 27		11 25	75	— 27	
Geo. Thompson	"	" 27		1 3	11.25	12 27		11 25	75	27	
Wm. Harris	"	" 27		1 3	11.25	12 27		11 25	75	27	
John McFarland	"	" 27		1 3	11.25	12 27		11 25	75	27	
Rufus Miller	"	" 27		1 3	11.25	12 27		11 25	75	27	
James Burns	"	" 27		1 3	11.25	12 27		11 25	75	27	
Jas. Harrison	"	" 27		1 3	11.25	12 27		11 25	75	27	
Daniel Leary	"	" 27		1 3	11.25	12 27		11 25	75	27	
Geo. Brun	"	" 27		1 3	11.25	12 27		11 25	75	27	
John Fee	"	" 27		1 3	11.25	12 27		11 25	75	27	
Wm. Scott	"	" 27		1 3	11.25	12 27		11 25	75	27	
Gilbert Ryan	"	" 27		1 3	11.25	12 27		11 25	75	27	
John Stephenson	"	" 27		1 3	11.25	12 27		11 25	75	27	
Daniel Vaughn	"	" 27		1 3	11.25	12 27		11 25	75	27	
Edwd. Inne	"	" 27		1 3	11.25	12 27		11 25	75	27	
Jas. McGinnis	"	" 27		1 3	11.25	12 27		11 25	75	27	
Jno. Williams	"	" 27		1 3	11.25	12 27		11 25	75	27	
Wm. Ayre	"	" 27		1 3	11.25	12 27		11 25	75	27	
Wm. Perry	"	" 27		1 3	11.25	12 27		11 25	75	27	But up 143.97
Thos. Carly	"	" 27		1 3	11.25	12 27		11 25	75	27	½ Cook 7 —
Wm. O'Neal	"	" 27		1 3	11.25	12 27		11 25	75	27	½ Mate 64.80
Jas. Addams	"	" 27		1 3	11.25	12 27		11 25	75	27	½ Seaman 50.91
Wm. Harrison	"	" 27		1 3	11.25	12 27		11 25	75	—	Wm. Robertshaw 26.10
Chas. Allen	"	" 27		1 3	11.25	12 27		11 25	75	27	2nd Mate 7.85
James Wilson	Ship Cook	" 27		1 3	11.25	12 27		11 25	75	27	305.63
Wm. Phillips	"	" 27		1 3	11.25	12 27		11 25	75	27	
						769 97	145 —	448 28	— 148 97		

*A **shipping document**, varying in size and content, generally defined as a statement made out by the shipmaster at the end of a voyage, which shows the total earnings of each member of the crew. The document debits the owners for the gross total earning of all on board, and credits them with any sums they may have advanced to any one of the officers or crew.*

Here is a small yet representative sample of the variety of receipts one might find in a collection of maritime manuscripts. These examples are particularly relevant to shipping, and would have been collected by the shipmaster during the course of his activity in port. Receipts can be productive research sources, and can yield valuable information about the business of shipping and the conduct of a vessel's affairs.

Entrance fees into the port of New Orleans, *$5.00, paid to the Port Warden, 22 June 1831.*

Having a ship towed into New Orleans, *$175.00, paid to the Steam Tow-Boat* Livingston, *22 June 1831.*

RECEIPTS

Receipt for hospital tax, *paid to the port Tax Collector, New Orleans, 2 June 1843. The Customs Service was required, after 1798, to collect a fee from all vessels arriving from foreign ports, based upon the number of crew members. The revenue was used to help establish and maintain hospitals and related services for sick or disabled seamen. This receipt indicates that a recent law passed in March, 1843, evidently revised or expanded the tax base.*

Harbor Master's fees *@ 3 cents per ton on the vessel, $6.36, paid to the Deputy Harbor Master, New Orleans, 22 June 1831. The Harbor Master enforced harbor regulations. He often controlled the mooring and berthing of ships, and scheduled the loading and discharge of cargo.*

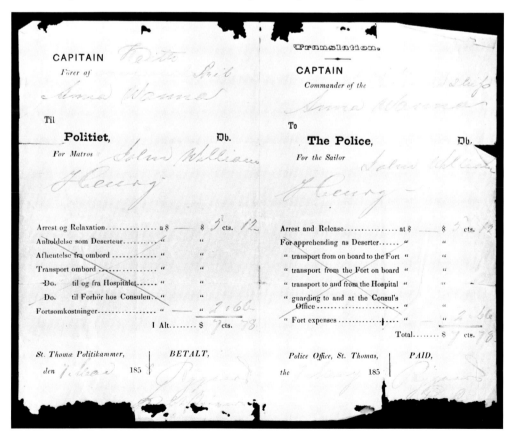

CUSTOM-HOUSE, NEW-YORK.

Brig Union

Permit to Unload, ... $	1	50
Harbor Master, ...	3	18
Health Officer, ...	3	
Hospital Money, ...	2	25
	$ 9 . 93	

Received Payment, *April 26* 1831

N Ogden
Cash

Customhouse services, $9.93, New York, 26 April 1831. The number of services rendered, and the amount for each, could vary from one vessel to another, and also between ports. Note that in this instance hospital monies and harbor masters fees were paid through the customhouse.

CAPITAIN *Fortie* *Skib*

Fører af

Anna Wanna

Til

Politiet, Db.

For Matros *John William*

Henry

Arrest og Relaxation. . . . . a $	$ 5 cts. 12
Anholdelse som Deserteur. . . . . "	"
Afhentelse fra ombord . . . . "	"
Transport ombord . . . . "	"
Do. til og fra Hospitalet. . . . . . "	"
Do. til Forhör hos Consulen. . "	"
Fortsomkostninger. . . . . "	2.66
I Alt. . . . . . . $	7 cts. 78

St. Thomæ Politikammer, | BETALT,

den *7 Mai* 185

Translation.

CAPTAIN *Skib*

Commander of the

Anna Wanna

To

The Police, Db.

For the Sailor *John William*

Henry

Arrest and Release. . . . . at $	$ 5 cts. 12
For apprehending as Deserter. . . . . . "	"
" transport from on board to the Fort "	"
" transport from the Fort on board "	"
" transport to and from the Hospital "	"
" guarding to and at the Consul's Office . . . . "	"
" Fort expenses . . . . "	2.66
Total. . . . . $	cts. 78

Police Office, St. Thomas, | PAID,

the *May* 185

The arrest and release of a sailor, $5.12, plus $2.66 "fort expenses," paid to the police of St. Thomas, V.I., 7 May 1858. The $5.12 would be deducted from the seaman's pay.

PORT OF BOSTON.

WHEREAS, the *Barque Austin* of *Boston* has arrived in the Port of Boston, with Alien Passengers on board who were never before within this Commonwealth: and whereas *D. W. Lord Consignee* of said vessel desires in lieu of the bond required by the first section of the Act of March 20, 1850, entitled "An Act relating to Alien Passengers," to pay to the Superintendent of Alien Passengers, for the use of the Commonwealth, the sum of two dollars for every such Alien, who *is* not in the opinion of the Superintendent, a pauper, lunatic or idiot, or maimed, aged, infirm or destitute, or incompetent to take care of himself, or herself, without becoming a public charge as a pauper. Now be it known, that I, *J. B. Munroe*, Superintendent of Alien Passengers, have this day received of the said *D. W. Lord* the sum of *Sixty four* Dollars in accordance with the said Act, and in pursuance of such *their* desire, and it is expressly understood and agreed by the said *D. W. Lord* that this payment or commutation is made at *his* request as voluntary, and never to be sued for, or recovered back in any process at law or in equity.

Superintendent of Alien Passengers,
59 Long Wharf.

Boston.

This receipt for 64 dollars indicates that 32 alien passengers were allowed to land at Boston, Massachusetts, in 1853, and it provides an example of an individual state's immigration laws during the mid-nineteenth century.

Whenever a vessel carrying alien passengers, or immigrants, arrived at a U.S. port, the master was required to report certain information to the municipal authorities. The regulations varied from state to state, but in general he was to report the names and places of residence or embarkation of these passengers to the selectmen, overseers of the poor, or mayor of the town. He then had to give a bond for each alien, to indemnify the town and state for any expenses that the immigrant might incur for his or her maintenance over a certain period of time. In Massachusetts, the value of the bond was one thousand dollars, and the time period covered was ten years. Other states averaged three to five hundred dollars bond value for a three to five year indemnification period. Masters of vessels were not required to give bond, however, when the officials saw fit either to dispense with the bond or to allow the master instead to pay a fee for each alien, as in the case of the document illustrated above. In Massachusetts this fee was two dollars, which was average for states that allowed the transaction. This landing fee was allowed when local authorities considered these passengers as unlikely to become public charges during the next several years. The document illustrated indicates that the master of the bark Austin apparently went to the city official in Boston, and, acting for the vessel's owner, D.W. Lord, received permission to pay the two-dollar landing fee for his promising group of passengers.

Printed document of various sizes, 19" x 16" was often used. Common format included an engraved scene with four sailing vessels near shore, centered at the top of the certificate. "United States" was engraved vertically along the left margin and topped by an eagle on a shield. "Register Of Vessels" was engraved in large print, vertically along the right margin. The signatures of the collector or deputy collector, and the port surveyor are usually present, as are various customs or consular seals.

The basic format for a Certificate of Registry was established by an Act of 31 December 1792, which prescribed numerous regulations for American shipping. The document was issued throughout the customs districts, to any American owned and built vessel over 20 tons, employed in foreign trade. It contained the vessel name, as well as the names of the owners and master. A physical description of the vessel was also included, along with the name of the place where she was built. A new Registration and a Register Bond was required whenever the vessel was physically altered (re-rigged, new deck house, etc.), or when her ownership changed. Permanent Registrations could only be secured at the vessel's official hailing port, although temporary certificates were issued when needed, by other custom's districts. Registers, and Enrolment Certificates, were made out in triplicate. One copy was given to the master for use aboard the vessel. A second copy was kept by the collector at the customhouse, while the third was sent to the Treasury Department. A number, usually found near the top of the document, complied with the 1792 Act, which required that each permanent and temporary certificate issued be numbered progressively, beginning anew each year. Ship's Registers were considered evidence of "national character," and most American vessels that qualified carried one. The document might be considered as serving the same general purpose as your automobile registration. They are fairly common maritime documents, although the fact that they were to be surrendered when no longer valid limits their numbers somewhat in private collections. They can provide valuable information for anyone involved in the study of a vessel's history and management.

REGISTRY CERTIFICATE/SHIP'S REGISTER

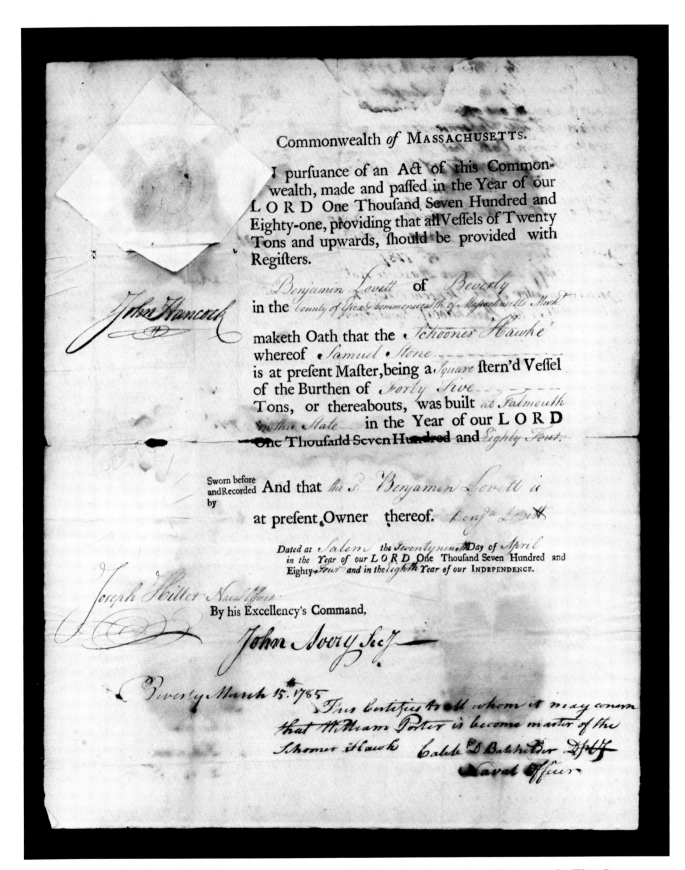

Commonwealth of MASSACHUSETTS.

IN pursuance of an Act of this Commonwealth, made and passed in the Year of our LORD One Thousand Seven Hundred and Eighty-one, providing that all Vessels of Twenty Tons and upwards, should be provided with Registers.

Benjamin Lovett of *Beverly* in the *County of Essex & Commonwealth of Massachusetts North*

maketh Oath that the *Schooner Hawke* whereof *Samuel Stone* is at present Master, being a *Square* stern'd Vessel of the Burthen of *Forty Five* Tons, or thereabouts, was built *at Falmouth in this State* in the Year of our LORD One Thousand Seven Hundred and *Eighty Four.*

Sworn before and Recorded by

And that *the sd Benjamin Lovett is* at present Owner thereof. *Benja Lovett*

Dated at *Salem* the *Twenty ninth* Day of *April* in the Year of our LORD One Thousand Seven Hundred and Eighty-*Four* and in the *eighth* Year of our INDEPENDENCE.

By his Excellency's Command,

John Avery Secy

Joseph Hiller Naval Officer

Beverly March 15th 1785. This certifies to all whom it may concern that William Porter is become master of the Schooner Hawke Caleb Batchelder D for Naval Officer

Before the Act of 1792, each state was responsible for registering and certifying vessels. This Certificate, issued by Massachusetts in accordance with state regulations passed by the Commonwealth in 1781, displays the state's seal and is signed by Governor John Hancock, 29 April 1784.

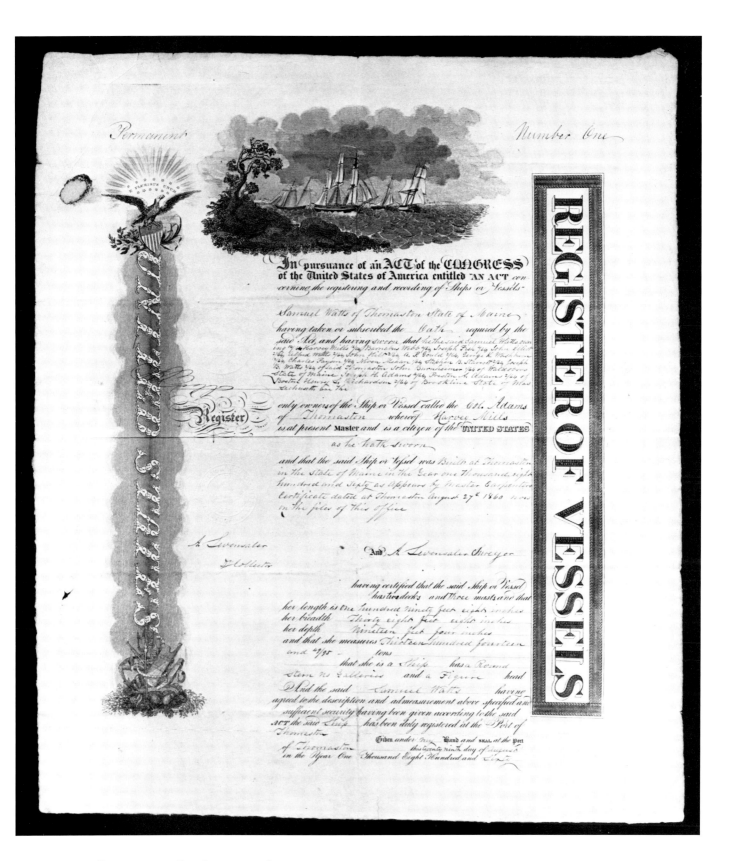

Permanent Register number one, *issued at the port of Thomaston, Maine, 29 August 1860. This was the first such document issued by that port during the year, and it was also the initial Register for the ship* Col. Adams, *whose construction had just been completed. Certificate displays customs seal and the signature of the collector.*

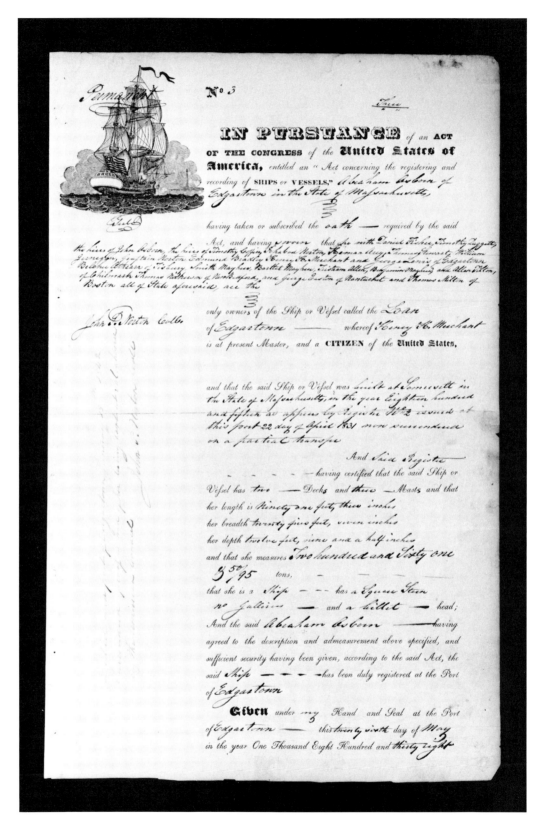

This is a record copy of a vessel's Registry Certificate, a document that was to be retained by the collector who issued the original. It is noticeably less ornate, but contains the same information. The margin notation on this copy, written by the collector, indicates that this ship was lost, and the original Registry Certificate surrendered at Talcahuano, Chile, in 1842, four years after the document was issued.

REGISTER BOND. *No.*

Know all Men by these Presents, That we,

Abraham Osborn, Henry H. Merchant and

are held and firmly bound to the United States of America, in the full and just sum of *two thousand* — — — — — Dollars; to which Payment, well and truly to be made, we bind Ourselves, our Heirs, Executors and Administrators, jointly and severally, by these Presents.

WITNESS our HANDS and SEALS, this *twenty eighth* — day of — — *May* . , in the Year one thousand eight hundred and thirty *eight* —

THE CONDITION of the foregoing Obligation is such, that whereas JOHN P. NORTON, Collector of the Customs for the District of *Edgartown*, has issued and granted a Certificate of Registry in the manner prescribed by the Act entitled "An Act concerning the registering and recording of ships and vessels," for the *ship* called the *Loan* — of *Edgartown* — burthen *261 59/95* — Tons, whereof *Henry H. Merchant* is at present Master, which Certificate is dated this day, and numbered *3*

Now THEREFORE, if the said Certificate of Registry shall be solely used for the said *Ship* — — — — — for which it has been granted; and shall not be sold, lent or otherwise disposed of to any person or persons whomsoever, and in case the said *Ship* — — — — shall be lost, or taken by an enemy, burnt or broken up, or shall be otherwise prevented from returning to the port to which she belongs; if the said Certificate (if preserved) shall within eight days after the arrival of the Master or person having the charge or command of the said *Ship* — — — — within any District of the United States, be delivered up to the Collector of such District; or if any Foreigner, or any person or persons for the use and benefit of such Foreigner, shall purchase or otherwise become entitled to the whole or any part or share of or interest in the said *Ship* — the same being within a District of the United States, if the said Certificate shall, within seven days after said purchase, change or transfer of property, be delivered up to the Collector of the said District;—or if such purchase, change or transfer of property shall happen when the said *Ship* — — — shall be at any foreign port or place, or at sea; if the Master or person having the charge or command thereof, shall, within eight days after his arrival within any District of the United States, deliver up said Certificate to the Collector of such District, then the said Obligation shall be void and of no effect; but otherwise shall remain in full force and virtue.

Signed, Sealed and Delivered,
in presence of

John P. Norton

Abm Osborn

Henry H. Merchant

Benjamin North

This Register Bond *was executed on the same day the Registry Certificate described previously was issued. The required document bonded the owners of the ship* Loan *to the U.S. government for a sum of two thousand dollars, as insurance for their compliance with conditions of the 1792 Act for registering and recording vessels.*

REGISTRY CERTIFICATE/SHIP'S REGISTER

District of the Port of Baltimore 2 [?]th Feby 1796

I hereby Certify that Andrew Boteler Master of the Schooner called the John of Alexandria Burthen sixty and $\frac{42}{95}$ths Tons; owned by James Cavan of Alexandria has surrendered to me, a certificate of Temporary Registry; granted to the said Schooner by R. Purviance Collector of the Customs for the District of Baltimore Numbered (250) and dated the 10th day of December 1795 — the vessels having been sold in Cape N. Mole

Given under my hand the day and year first above written

Collector

This certificate, signed by the collector at the Port of Baltimore on 26 February 1796, is a receipt indicating that the master of the schooner John had properly given up the Temporary Registry Certificate issued to the vessel at Baltimore 10 weeks earlier. Since the John had been sold, a new permanent registry was required. Certificates similar in size and style were also issued for receipt of vessel Enrollments.

Custom House, Boston,

Collector's Office, *Mar 11* 1856

Sir:

The *S. Register* No. *100*
granted for the *Bark Austin 15 mai*
18*48* is unaccounted for, as appears by the Records of this Office.

You are requested to fill up the annxed Answer with any
information you may have relative to the said vessel, or her papers,
that the Books of the Treasury Department, at Washington, may
be cancelled.

I am, respectfully,
Your Obedient Servant,

C. H. Peabu Collector.

To *Daniel W Leach Esq*

*Kennebunkport,
My*

This form letter from the collector at Boston indicates the extent to which the customs districts sought to control the circulation of Ship's Registers and Enrollments.

SAILING CARD

Often printed on heavy grade card stock, 4" x 6 1/2" being a common size. Many examples feature elaborately engraved scenes, and contain as many as seven different colors. The reverse side is usually blank.

Sailing Cards and announcements are not truly manuscript items; however, they are significant and distinctive maritime documents. Agents or owners commonly advertised the availability and loading of their vessels in the local newspapers, but by the mid-1850s the colorful Sailing Cards began to appear in the windows of shipping firms, banks, and public shops along the waterfronts in ports like New York and Boston. These cards might be printed several days prior to the anticipated departure, in order to secure last-minute cargo or passengers. Initially a specific sailing date was not included on the card, although some later examples do state that the ship would sail "on or about" a certain day. Sailing Cards then, are difficult to date accurately, but it seems that many of the vessels represented on these eye-catching advertisements flourished between the 1850s and the 1880s. Many of the early card announcements were used primarily to advertise sailings to California following the discovery of gold there in 1849. Consequently, I have heard them often referred to as "Clipper Ship Sailing Cards." Evidence would indicate, however, that they continued to be used long after the preeminence of the Clipper (and gold fever) had passed. Despite this lengthy period of use, Sailing Cards are relatively scarce. They are popular collectables, and frequently command a high value in the open market.

Sailing Card for the "New York built Clipper Ship Enterprise" *reveals the highly detailed engraving often found on these announcements.*

SAILING ORDERS

A handwritten manuscript, *varying in size and composition, which detailed a shipmaster's responsibilities for an upcoming voyage. These orders were usually signed by the vessel's agents or owners. The master's signature might also appear, indicating that he had read, and/or received his copy of the document. Notary stamps or customs seals are not present since this was essentially a private agreement between the two parties. Formal instructions were not always necessary, and might depend on the shipmaster's relationship with his employers, or even his financial interest in the vessel he commanded.*

Sailing Orders are occasionally found in maritime collections, They are always important research sources, often providing insight into the broadly defined range of responsibilities that the master of a merchant vessel might assume during his voyage. He could be required to do much more than get his ship quickly and safely from one port to another, frequently buying or selling cargo, and otherwise managing the ship's business until the voyage was completed. Illustrated is the Sailing Orders given to Captain Paraclete Holmes of the ship Helen Mar, for a voyage from New York to New Orleans, 1830. He was instructed, in part, to assist in procuring "all the freight in your power and also cabin and steerage passengers." Upon his arrival at New Orleans, he was to work with assigned agents there to get "a return freight for Boston," oversee its stowage, and pay all the ship's bills before departure. In return, Holmes received 40 dollars per month, plus 5% "passage money" and an extra 5% primage on the total value of the homeward freight.

Seamen's Protection Certificates were usually printed documents, varying in size and style, that were carried by American seamen as proof of citizenship. The certificate was obtained by the individual through the customhouse, public notary, or U.S. Consul when required in a foreign port. It contained the person's name, birthplace, approximate age, height, skin color, eye and hair color, and other distinctive descriptive information, such as the location of scars or tattoos. "United States of America" was often printed prominently across the top, and the word "protection" might also appear. Small engravings of the American eagle often served to decorate and establish the nationality of the document. A serial number was included on every Customs Protection Certificate for recordkeeping purposes. The wording of the document was standardized, having been transcribed on many examples, verbatim from the Act of 1796.

The Act of 28 May 1796, entitled "An Act for the Protection and Relief of American Seamen," provided certificates for the protection of American seamen from the threat of impressment by the Royal Navy. Prior to this act, a mariner could obtain a similar document from a public notary. An individual desiring protection was required to bring some authenticated proof of citizenship to the customs collector, who, for a service fee of 25 cents, would issue him a certificate. Most seamen of the day, however, were so transient that they were unable to produce the required proof, and so the condition was altered to allow him to bring a notarized affidavit, instead, in which the seamen and a witness swore to his citizenship. Because it was easy to abuse this system, the Royal Navy did not always honor the Protection Certificates as valid. Collectors were required to keep a record book of the names of individuals receiving protections and send quarterly lists to the State Department. As the threat to American freedom on the high seas began to disappear, Protection Certificates became more valuable as identification, and they were used as such until 1940, when the Seamen's Continuous Discharge Book replaced them. These documents are common items in maritime collections and are important research sources for any study of American seamen.

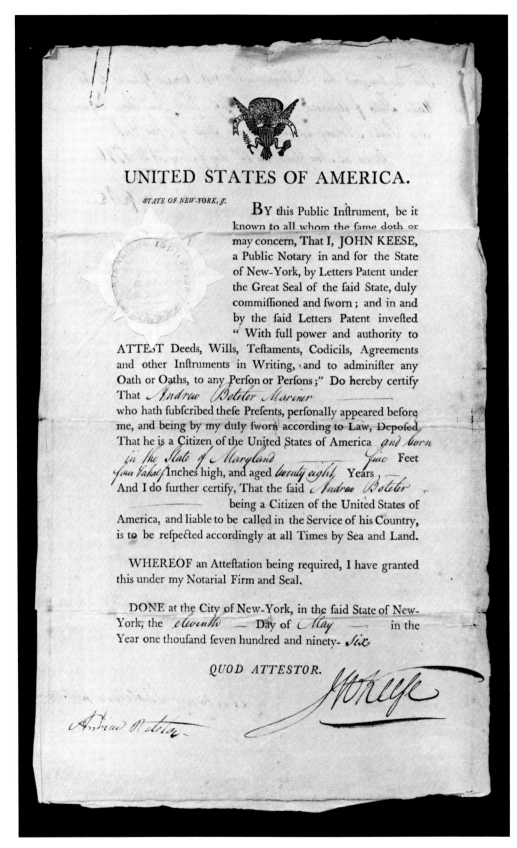

Notary Protection Certificate *issued to Andrew Boteler, mariner, 11 May 1796. Dated seventeen days before the passage of the Act that prescribed use of Seamen's Protections, it served the same purpose. A document such as this would later often be required by the collector in order for a seaman to obtain a certificate from the Custom House.*

PROTECTION.

UNITED STATES OF AMERICA.

State of Massachusetts.　　　No. *1317*　　　District of New Bedford.

I, C. B. H. FESSENDEN, Collector of the District aforesaid, do hereby Certify, That *George H. Reynolds* an AMERICAN SEAMAN, aged *23* years, or thereabouts, of the height of *5* feet *9¼* inches, *dark* complexion *dark* hair, *blue* eyes, born at

New York City

has this day produced to me proof in the manner directed in the Act entitled "An Act for the relief and protection of American Seamen," and, pursuant to the said Act, I do hereby Certify, That the said *George H. Reynolds* is a Citizen of the United States of America.

In Witness Whereof, I have hereunto set my hand and seal of Office, this *6* day of *October* in the year of our Lord one thousand eight hundred and fifty-*nine*

C. B. H. Fessenden Collector.

This certificate, issued through the Custom House in New Bedford, Massachusetts, is typical in many ways of Seamen's Protections used throughout the period. These documents, like many others, were created by local printers, so that variations in style and dimensions are evident when comparing pieces used at various ports.

UNITED STATES OF AMERICA,
STATE OF TEXAS.

BY THIS PUBLIC INSTRUMENT,

Be it known to all whom the same doth or may concern, That *I E. P. Hunt a* **PUBLIC NOTARY**, *in and for the City and County of Galveston, do hereby certify that Jonathan Miller who now personally appears before me, is aged about twenty three years.*

Height *5 feet 7 inches*	Scars
Complexion *Black*	By Profession *Seaman*
Hair *Woolly*	Born in *New York*

In the United States of America, all of which has been duly proven to my satisfaction. I do, therefore, further certify, that he is a freeman and a citizen of the United States of America, and entitled to be respected accordingly in person and property, at all times and places, both by sea and land, in the due prosecution of his lawful concerns.

In Witness Whereof, *I have caused my Notarial Seal of Office to be hereunto affixed, at the City of Galveston, the twenty second day of January in the year of our Lord one thousand eight hundred and Fifty Six.*

E. P. Hunt
Notary Public

This Protection certifies the citizenship and freedom of Jonathan Miller, a black seaman, issued at Galveston, Texas, in 1856. Provided by a public notary, this form was probably more significant for its protection of Miller's freedom in the South, i.e. "by sea and land" than for its maritime use.

SHIPBUILDING AGREEMENTS AND CONTRACTS

These were usually handwritten documents, varying in size, containing a detailed description of the obligations and responsibilities of all parties involved in the contract. These "Agreements" might be concluded between an owner and a shipyard, to cover the construction of a vessel, or it could be written for specific work such as rigging, iron work, etc. Included are the signatures of both parties, as well as required witnesses to the agreement. Some documents may display notary stamps or seals, but this was evidently not generally required.

Illustrated above are Shipbuilding Agreements typical of the kind often found in manuscript collections from the nineteenth century. On the left is a portion of a four-page document for the construction of a ship at the agreed rate of forty dollars per ton. The contract on the right is a rigging agreement for $437.00.

STEAMBOAT REGULATORY DOCUMENTS

In 1838, amidst increasing steamboat accidents and passenger fatalities, the Federal government got involved by passing "An Act to provide for the better security of passengers on board vessels propelled in whole or in part by steam." The Act called for some loosely worded regulations, including the creation of inspectors for steam vessels—particularly the hulls, boilers, and related machinery. An inspector or inspectors were to be appointed for each port by the local Federal district court judge. The inspectors were in charge of inspecting and, in turn, certifying steam vessels that operated out of their port.

Accidents still occurred and safety standards continued to lag. Consequently, in August, 1852, Congress passed an amendment to the 1838 Act which included tougher legislation, and created an elaborate structure for its implementation. Nine supervising inspectors were appointed by the President of the United States to oversee all districts listed in the amendment. Hull and boiler inspectors were then appointed within each district, and it became their responsibility to examine and certify all aspects of steam vessels as well as to license steam engineers and steam pilots.

This amendment not only established certifying requirements for vessels, pilots, and engineers, but it also created the specific wording of the documents themselves. By 1858 the Steamboat Regulatory Certificates had become fairly uniform in style and content.

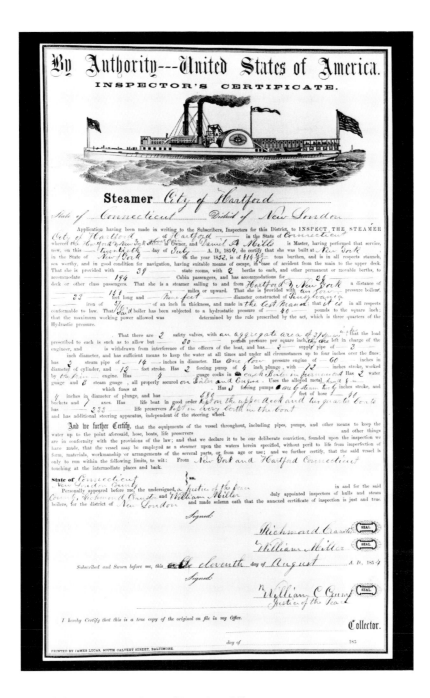

Inspector's Certificate/Hull & Boiler Certificate: *Large printed document, approximately 10" x 16" being a common size. Title is printed prominently near the top and many examples feature decorative engraving. Certificates often begin with the phrase, "Application having been made in writing to the subscribers; Inspectors for said district, to inspect the Steamer. . ." At bottom places are provided for the signatures of the inspectors (hull and boiler), the collector, and a Justice of the Peace or other notary. Various stamps or seals may also appear.*

This document, often called a Hull & Boiler Certificate, was a product of Federal legislation begun in 1838 to better regulate the safety of steam vessels and their machinery, and was issued after a thorough examination of the ship, including the hull, passenger accommodations, boilers, safety equipment, and life boats had been successfully completed. It defined the geographical limits within which that particular steamboat may operate, i.e. "From New York and Hartford, Connecticut, touching at intermediate places and back." The original was filed with the collector, and copies given to the owner/operators of the vessel. Copies of this certificate were to be prominently displayed aboard the vessel, which was reinspected periodically depending upon the conditions of service.

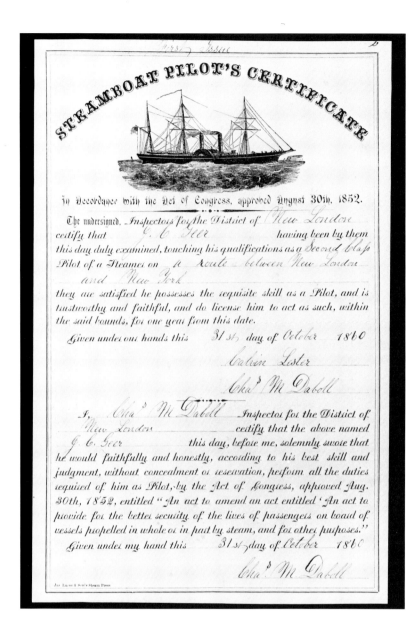

Steamboat Pilot's Certificate: *A one-page printed document, prior to 1860 a common size was 6 1/2" x 10 1/2". "Steamboat Pilot's Certificate" is often printed boldly across the top. Most documents have printed or engraved borders, and some exhibit a detailed engraving of a three-masted side-wheel steamship, centered in the upper portion of the certificate. Similar in form to the Engineer's Certificate, the Steamboat Pilot's Certificate also carries the name and rating of the pilot, along with an oath, swearing that he will comply with the Congressional Act of 1852 regarding the supervision of steamboats and their machinery. Issued through local customs districts, the license usually contained the signatures of the inspectors and the collector.*

The Steamboat Pilot's Certificate became a requirement after the amendment to existing steamboat legislation was passed in 1852. Steam pilots were thus federally regulated, while those aboard sailing vessels could remain, for a while at least, under the supervision of individual states. The pilot candidate was examined by the inspectors for his knowledge and qualifications regarding the specific waterway he intended to work. License was valid for one year.

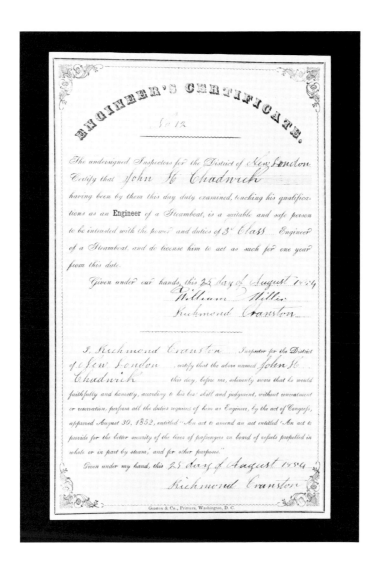

Engineer's Certificate: *A one-page printed document, often with decorative engraved border and "Engineer's Certificate" printed boldly across the top. Spaces provided for the engineer's name and rating i.e. 1st class, 3rd class, etc. Signatures of the district's hull and boiler inspectors, along with the date of execution, appear near the bottom of the license, which is valid for a period of one year. Common dimensions for this period were approximately 6 1/2" x 10 1/2". Customs or notary seals were evidently not required.*

In 1852, an amendment to the existing Federal steamboat legislation required that engineers be certified as specified in the amendment. It was the duty of an engineer to maintain and operate, or in the case of a first engineer, supervise the maintenance and operation, of the steamboat's machinery. Once licensed into a certain class, the engineer could then hire himself out to work on a steam vessel.

Printed document, varying in size and format, *usually found on a single sheet of heavy grade paper of fairly large proportions. "Whalemen's Shipping Paper" was often printed across the top, with some examples displaying eagles, shields, ribbons, etc., engraved along the upper margin. Conditions of the agreement for the voyage were printed on the front side of the document. Columns are included for a crew member's signature, date signed, his position aboard ship, his share of the voyage, and for witnesses' signatures. Columns for other data may also appear. Pertinent sections of Federal legislation for the protection of American seamen, usually including the original Act of 1790, are quite often found printed on the backside of these papers. Customs or consular stamps and seals will be present on some examples.*

The Whalemen's Shipping Paper was used by the whaling industry in the same way as Articles of Agreement were by the merchant fleet, significant differences being the specific conditions for a whaling voyage, which were read and agreed to by the individual signing the paper; and the column for "shares," the fraction written there indicating the proportion of total revenue from the upcoming voyage that represented the crewman's wages. Since these documents were printed locally at the various ports there is little standardization in size or content, but examples that are completely filled out and well-preserved prove to be valuable and interesting research sources.

SELECTED LIST OF U.S. STATUTES RELATIVE TO THE FEDERAL REGULATION OF AMERICAN SHIPPING: 1789-1860

1789 Three acts passed in July creating U.S. Customs Service.

1789 Chapter IX, Section 4. An act for regulation of pilots.

1790 Chapter XXIX, Sections 1 through 9. Act for the government and regulation of Seamen in the Merchant Service; contracts with crew, desertions and required provisions.

1792 Chapter XXIV, Sections 1 through 6 and Section 9 (Sections 7 & 8 repealed). Act concerning Consuls and Vice-Consuls concerning powers and duties. (Established U.S. Consular Service).

1792 Chapter I, Sections 1 through 30. Act for registering, recording and clearing vessels.

1793 Chapter VIII, Sections 1 through 37. Act for enrolling and licensing ships or vessels in the coasting trade and fisheries and regulating same. This act includes laws pertaining to cargo manifests.

1796 Chapter XXXVI, Chapters 1 through 8. Act for the relief and protection of United States seamen including appointment of agents to act on behalf of said seamen in case of impressment or detention by a foreign power.

1796 Chapter XLV, Sections 1 through 4. Act providing passports for ships and vessels.

1797 Chapter VII. Act concerning registering and recording ships or vessels and licensing ships and vessels in the coasting trade and fisheries in the case of lawful sale or transfer.

1797 Chapter V. Act concerning registry and recording of ships and vessels in the event of seizure or capture by a foreign power, or by sale become the property of a foreigner.

1798 Chapter LXXVII, Sections 1 through 5. Act concerning relief of sick and disabled seamen including fees and regulations for hospitals.

1802 Chapter LI, Sections 1 through 7. Amendment of Act for relief of sick and disabled seamen which provides for relief of foreign seamen.

1803 Chapter IX, Sections 1 through 8. Act concerning Consuls and Vice Consuls, and for further protection of American seamen.

1803 Chapter XVI, Sections 1 and 2. Supplement to act providing passports for vessels of the United States.

1803 Chapter XVIII, Sections 1 through 4. An act in addition to the act concerning registering and recording of vessels of the United States and to regulate the collection of duties on imports and tonnage.

1804 Chapter LII, Sections 1 and 2. Act to amend the act concerning registering and recording of vessels.

1805 Chapter XXVIII. An act to amend the Act of 1790, Chapter XXIX, Section eight, an act concerning regulation of seamen in the Merchant's Service.

1810 Chapter XIX. Act to prevent the issuing of Sea Letters to certain vessels.

1811 Chapter XXVIII. An act in addition to the Act of 1803, Chapter IX concerning Consuls and Vice-Consuls and protection of American seamen.

1812 Chapter XL, Sections 1 and 2. Act concerning enrolling and licensing of steamboats.

1813 Chapter XLII, Sections 1 through 14. Act for regulation of seamen on board public and private vessels of the United States, concerning citizenship of such seamen.

1813 Chapter II, Sections 1 and 2. Act for the government of persons in certain fisheries regulating employment of fishermen and shares of proceeds of fishing voyages.

1817 Chapter XXXI, Sections 1 through 7. Act concerning navigation of the United States to regulate imports from foreign ports, citizenship requirements for crews on fishing vessels and trade between U.S. ports.

1819 Chapter LXXXVII, Sections 1. Act to protect the commerce of the United States, and punish the crime of piracy.

1825 Chapter XCIX, Sections 1 through 5. An act to authorize the register or enrolment and license to be issued in the name of the president or secretary of any incorporated company owning a steamboat or vessel.

1830 Chapter XIV, Sections 1 and 2. Act to authorize surveyors, under the direction of the Secretary of the Treasury, to enroll and license ships or vessels to be employed in the coasting trade and fisheries.

1831 Chapter XCVIII, Sections 1 through 4. Act to regulate the foreign and coasting trade on the northern, north-eastern and north-western frontiers of the United States.

1831 Chapter CXV. Act concerning vessels employed in the whale fishery concerning register or enrolment and license.

1837 Chapter XXII. Act concerning employment of pilots.

1838 Chapter CXCI, Sections 1 through 13. Act to provide for the security of the lives of passengers on board steam-propelled vessels, and inspection of these vessels.

1840 Chapter VI, Sections 1 through 3. Act to cancel the bonds to secure duties upon vessels and their cargoes, employed in the whale fishery, and to make registers lawful papers.

1840 Chapter XLVIII. Act regulating the shipment and discharge of seamen, and the duties of consuls.

1843 Chapter XLIX. Act amending the act for the relief of sick and disabled seamen to be extended to masters, owners and seamen of vessels in the coasting trade.

1843 Chapter XCIV, Sections 1 through 6. Act to modify the Act of 1838, Chapter CXCI, to provide for the better security of the lives of passengers on board steam vessels.

1848 Chapter CXLI, Sections 1 through 3. Act to authorize the Secretary of the Navy to license yachts used as pleasure vessels.

1850 Chapter XXVII, Sections 1 through 8. Act to provide for recording conveyances and sales of vessels.

1851 Chapter XLIII, Sections 1 through 7. Act to limit liability of ship owners, and to make charters of vessels liable in same manner as owners.

1852 Chapter CVI, Sections 1 through 44. Act to amend the act to provide for the better security of the lives of passengers on board steam vessels, regulating inspection, safety measures and licensing of such vessels.

1852 Chapter CXIII, Section 5. Act regulating delivery of U.S. mail carried on ships.

1852 Chapter IV. Act authorizing the Secretary of the Treasury to issue registers in certain cases.

1855 Chapter CXXXIII, Sections 15 through 20. Act to remodel the diplomatic and consular systems of the United States.

1855 Chapter CCXIII, Sections 1 through 19. Act to regulate the carriage of passengers in steamships and other vessels, including those employed by the American Colonization Society, or such society of any state, to transport colored emigrants to the coast of Africa.

1856 Chapter CXXVII, Sections 20, 25 through 28. Act supplementary to the Act of 1803, concerning Consuls and Vice-Consuls and for the further protection of American seamen, and to provide for discharge and desertion of seamen.

Abbott, Charles. *A Treatise of Law Relative to Merchant Ships & Seamen.* Newburyport: E. Little & Co., 1810.

Allen, Edward L. *Pilot Lore; From Sail to Steam.* New York: 1922.

American Bureau of Shipping; 75th Anniversary, 1862-1937. New York: A.B.S., 1937.

American Shipmaster's Daily Assistant. Portland: 1807.

Baker, Albert S. *Morning Stars & Missionary Packet.* Honolulu: 1945.

Bishop, John A. *Suggestions to Masters of Vessels in Case of Disaster.* [h.p. 1903].

Blunt, Joseph. *Merchant's & Shipmaster's Assistant.* N.Y.: E & G.W. Blunt, 1822. (Various editions).

Buglass, Leslie J. *Marine Insurance & General Average in the U.S.* Cambridge, Md: Cornell Maritime Press, 1973.

Burney, William Dr. *Falconer's Marine Dictionary.* London: 1815.

Butts, Isaac Ridler. *The Businessman's Assistant.* Boston: I.R. Butts, 1847.

Butts, Isaac Ridler. *Law of the Sea.* Boston: I.R. Butts, 1849.

Butts, Isaac Ridler. *The Merchant's Shipmaster's & Mates Manual...*Boston: I.R. Butts, 1855.

Butts, Isaac Ridler. *The Merchant's & Mechanic's Assistant.* Boston: I.R. Butts, 1858.

Clark, Francis G. *American Shipmaster's Guide & Commercial Assistant.* Boston: Allen & Co., 1838.

Clark, William Bell ed. *Naval Documents of the American Revolution.* Washington: U.S. Government Printing Office, 1964.

Clauder, Anna Cornelia. *American Commerce As Affected By the Wars of the French Revolution & Napoleon, 1793-1812.* Clifton, N.J.: A.M. Kelly, 1972.

Coggeshall, George. *History of the American Privateers & Letters-of-Marque...* New York; 1856.

Cranwell, John Phillips. *Men of Marque...* New York: W.W. Norton & Co., 1940.

Custom House Souvenir of the Port of New York. 1893-94.

Dana, Richard Henry. *The Seamen's Friend.* 3d ed. Boston, Little & Brown, 1844.

de Kerchove, Rene. *International Maritime Dictionary.* 2d ed. New York: Van Nostrand Reinhold Co., 1983.

Dixon, Francis B. *The Law of Shipping.* New York: H. Spear, 1859.

Dixon, Francis B. *Handbook of Marine Insurance & Average.* New York: H. Spear, 1862.

Dudley, William S. ed. *The Naval War of 1812, A Documentary History.* Vol. 1. Washington, D.C.: Naval Historical Center, 1985.

Dye, Ira. "Seafarers of 1812 - A Profile." Prologue: Spring, 1973.

Dye, Ira. "The Philadelphia Seamen's Protection Certificate Applications." Prologue: Spring, 1986.

Forbes, Allan. *Yankee Ship Sailing Cards.* 3 vols. Boston, Ma: State Street Trust Co., 1948-1952.

Garitee, Jerome R. *The Republic's Private Navy.* Mystic, Ct.: Mystic Seaport Museum, 1977.

A History of the Marine Society at Salem. Salem, Massachusetts: The Marine Society at Salem, 1966.

Homan, Isaac Smith. *A Cyclopedia of Commerce & Commercial Navigation.* N.Y.: Harper & Bros., 1858.

Huebner, Salomon Stephen. *Marine Insurance.* New York: D. Appleton & Co., 1920.

La Boyteaux, William Harvell. *Handbook For Masters.* New York: 1919.

McCulloch, J. *A Dictionary, Practical, Theoretical, & Historical, of Commerce & Navigation.* 2 vols. Philadelphia: Carey & Hart, 1847.

Miller, William J. *Encyclopedia of International Commerce.* Centerville, Md.: Cornell Maritime Press, 1985.

Montefiore, Joshua. *A Commercial Dictionary.* 3 vols. Philadelphia: James Humphreys, 1804.

Montefiore, Joshua. *The American Trader's Compendium.* Philadelphia: S.R. Fisher, 1811.

Morgan, William James. "American Privateering in America's War For Independence, 1775-1783". *American Neptune.* April, 1976.

Naval Documents Related To The U.S. Wars With the Barbary Powers. 4 vols. U.S. Government Printing Office, 1939.

Niles Weekly Register. Baltimore, 1811-1849.

Parsons, Theophilus. *A Treatise On Maritime Law.* 2 vols. Boston: Little, Brown & Co., 1859.

Prince, Carl E. *The U.S. Customs Service: A Bicentennial History.* Washington D.C.: Dept. of the Treasury, 1989.

Register of Approved Shipmasters. N.Y., 1865.

Rubin, Israel Ira. *New York State & The Long Embargo.* Dissertation, N.Y. University, 1962.

Serene, Frank H. "American Immigrant Genealogy: Ship Passenger Lists". Prologue: Summer, 1985.

Sullivan, Eric. *The Marine Encyclopedic Dictionary.* Valetta, Malta: Gulf Publishing Co., 1980.

U.S. Congress, *The New American State Papers: Commerce & Navigation, 1789-1860.* 47 vols. Wilmington, Delaware, Scholarly Resources, 1973.

The U.S. Consular System: A Manual For Consuls... Washington: Taylor & Maury, 1856 ed.

U.S. Nautical Magazine & Naval Journal. 7 vols. N.Y., O.W. Griffiths, Monthly, Oct. 1854-Mar. 1858.

Warren, June S. *The Morning Star: A History of the Children's Missionary Vessel...*Boston: American Tract Soc., 1860.

Wynkoop, Richard. *Vessels & Voyages.* New York: D. Van Nostrand, 1887.

AMERICAN MARITIME DOCUMENTS 1776-1860

Typeset in Baskerville by Thames Printing Co., Inc.,
Norwich, Connecticut

Printed on Warren Lustro Dull creme text paper

Printed and bound by Thomson-Shore, Inc.,
Dexter, Michigan

Designed by Barbara Rogan, Stonington Design,
Mystic, Connecticut